THIS BOOK BELONGS TO
The Library of

....

....

©COPYRIGHT 2024

The content contained within this book may not be reproduced, duplicated, or transmitted without direct written permission from the author or the publisher. Under no circumstances will any blame or legal responsibility be held against the publisher, or author, for any damages, reparation, or monetary loss due to the information contained within this book. Either directly or indirectly.

Legal Notice:

This book is copyright protected. This book is only for personal use. You cannot amend, distribute, sell, use, quote, or paraphrase any part, or the content within this book, without the consent of the author or publisher.

Disclaimer Notice:

Please note the information contained within this document is for educational and entertainment purposes only. All effort has been executed to present accurate, up-to-date, and reliable, complete information. No warranties of any kind are declared or implied. Readers acknowledge that the author is not engaging in the rendering of legal, financial, medical, or professional advice. The content within this book has been derived from various sources. Please consult a licensed professional before attempting any techniques outlined in this book. By reading this document, the reader agrees that under no circumstances is the author responsible for any losses, direct or indirect, which are incurred as a result of the use of the information contained within this document, including, but not limited to — errors, omissions, or inaccuracies.

Thank you for Purchasing my book and taking the time to read it from front to back. I am always grateful when a reader chooses my work and I hope you enjoyed it!

With the vast selection available online, I am touched that you chose to be purchasing my work and take valuable time out of your life to read it. My hope is that you feel you made the right decision.

I very much would like to know what you thought of the book. Please take the time to write an honest and informative review on Amazon.com. Your experience and opinions will be of great benefit to me and those readers looking to make an informed choice.

With much thanks.

Table of Contents

Chapter 1: Welcome to Lisbon — 9

Chapter 2: Enjoy Lisbon Throughout the Year — 17

Chapter 3: Top Sights, Streets, and Secrets of the City — 24

Chapter 4: Taste the Flavors of the City — 36

Chapter 5: Where to Stay and Settle — 43

Chapter 6: Travel and Transport — 52

Chapter 7: Discover Lisbon's Natural Beauty — 60

Chapter 8: Traveling During Covid-19 — 71

Chapter 9: Local Lisbon Living — 75

Conclusion — 79

References — 84

Introduction

Travel and exploration are great for the mind and soul. Traveling to a foreign country can be exciting but also very stressful. There is so much planning involved and this can get in the way of seeing the joy that comes with traveling, yet this does not need to be the case for you. It is possible to have a great European trip with little to no worries by planning and preparing beforehand. Learning about the country you are going to visit and knowing your travel wish list will make it easier for you to enjoy your holiday when you arrive at your destination. Therefore, this travel guide will be your best friend while you plan your trip to Lisbon.

In this guide, you will learn about the Portuguese city of Lisbon and how you can have an unforgettable holiday in this beautiful European paradise. While some incredible experiences can come from spontaneous adventures, there is always a need for preparation when it comes to going on a trip to a different country. This is why in Chapter 1, there will be a brief background on Lisbon as well as a discussion on how to travel around the city with some smart travel tips and hacks. This chapter will provide the information you need to travel around the city with ease while avoiding tourist traps. There will also be a section dedicated to learning how to create your very own itinerary to ensure that you have the holiday of your dreams in Lisbon.

Chapter 2 will guide you through the annual activities, events, and festivals that occur in and around Lisbon. Here, you will be able to have a calendar-like guide to follow and learn about what is happening in the city during the time of your trip. You could also decide when you would like to travel to Lisbon based on this calendar. We will also go through the seasonal events that take place in the city, from summer to spring. No matter what season or day, there is always something for you to do in Lisbon and we will help you find that special activity, attraction, or event that is perfect for you!

When we think of attractions in Lisbon, there are many historical sights to see like churches and museums as well as old buildings, but there are also more local attractions or must-see places that are less known yet just as special. In Chapter 3, we will provide you with several lists of attractions that you could try out and enjoy on your trip. From tourist attractions to hidden gems and side streets, there is so much for you to explore and admire in Lisbon, places you may never have imagined.

From attractions to dining out, Lisbon has got it all and these places are just waiting for you to experience all that they offer. In Chapter 4, we will look at some of the best restaurants and culinary experiences that you can find in Lisbon. From fine dining, to more family-friendly restaurants, to kitchens and delis and even unique culinary experiences for the foodies, we have got it all here for you to take your pick. This chapter will get you excited about tasting the traditional and contemporary flavors at many establishments located in Lisbon. Depending on your food preferences, budget, and palate, we have compiled lists of the best places for you to sit, socialize, and savor the flavors and culinary atmosphere of Lisbon.

Chapter 5 will help you out with your accommodation needs. Here, we have covered different types of accommodations at different prices to help you find the best place to get some rest and relaxation. Lisbon is not just for a short stay, but it is a great place to settle down. Yes, Lisbon is good for expats to make a new or second home in. This is why this chapter breaks down the many types of stays one can find in this area of Portugal. From the best hotels, budget-friendly hostels, homestays, and even family-friendly or retirement neighborhoods, we have got it covered in this chapter.

The next chapter will give you necessary tips about traveling across the city, specifically on the different modes of transport that are available in Lisbon. From intra-city transport to different routes in and out of the city, Chapter 6 will give you the information you will need to become an expert at daily travel around Lisbon. Depending on your length of stay, your budget, and transport preferences, you can choose the mode of transport that works for you.

While transportation amenities are important when planning a trip, the streets and trails of the city are just as important when you are wanting to make unforgettable memories. Chapter 7 is dedicated to the many outdoor activities you can try out to experience the natural beauty of Lisbon's landscape. The city life is great, but Lisbon also offers outdoor experiences if you are looking for some unique adventures. In and around the city, there are many beaches and nature reserves in the region. In this chapter, we will provide some popular beaches as well as some more isolated, serene places you can visit while in the Lisbon region.

To navigate the city, you also need to know some travel limitations, especially due to the current Covid-19 pandemic. Therefore, Chapter 8 will discuss the updated Portuguese Covid-19 protocol that needs to be followed as well as the travel policies that have been implemented by the local and national governments. Social norms and formal policies are important when trying to assimilate into a foreign city.

Following on from this discussion, Chapter 9 will cover the social norms and unwritten cultural rules of Portuguese living. Whether your stay in Lisbon will last two weeks, a month or several months, learning about the local culture is very important and will only make your stay richer and more enjoyable. Becoming part of the community involves learning the language and culture of the place as well as being aware of the dos and don'ts of the society, which this chapter will highlight. Your stay in Lisbon can be a unique and special trip as you make it perfect for you. Your travel dreams can come true with some planning, an open and adventurous mind, and of course, and learning from this guide. Now, let us begin making your Lisbon journey come to life!

Chapter 1: Welcome to Lisbon

A Brief Background of the City

Portugal is a popular holiday destination and attracts many tourists from all over the world. The country offers so much, from city life to historical buildings and even so many natural attractions like its many stunning beaches and iconic hills. This is why Lisbon is the most-visited city in Portugal as it offers city-living with nightlife and busy streets as well as more quaint beaches and nature reserves outside the city. Lisbon, a coastal city, is a hub of culture and draws people from all over the world. While there are many tourist-dominated places, Lisbon still preserves its authentic Portuguese flair in its own unique way.

This city is a place where old meets new as traditions are kept and contemporary sites are also introduced to the locals and tourists alike. Lisbon is the largest city in Portugal and is one of the oldest and most lively cities you will find in Europe. The architecture showcases the many decades, centuries of art, history, and culture that have come out of this city, which is displayed by the grand São Jorge Castle or the vistas of Alfama. As you walk through the city, you can find cobbled streets with old-world homes that still stand today, but walk a bit further, and you will discover contemporary buildings and trendy cafés.

The city has seen so many historical events and has withstood the test of time. From both World Wars to the fascism that was upheld by António Salazar up until the 1970s, the struggles, movements, and cultural resets have made this Portuguese city what it is today. Today, the people of Lisbon celebrate freedom and liberation with passion and energy. You can see this shared zest for life in the many traditions, customs, events, and establishments across the city.

Due to the culture of the locals, the natural beauty of the city, and of course the pleasant Mediterranean climate, many people flock to Lisbon for holidays, work, or long-term stays every year. Lisbon is the capital city of Portugal, and this means that it is the most populated and the most visited by tourists. Planning a trip to Lisbon is much more exciting and easier than you think due to the tourist-friendly culture and systems put in place. This city really is a hub and has something special waiting for every type of traveler.

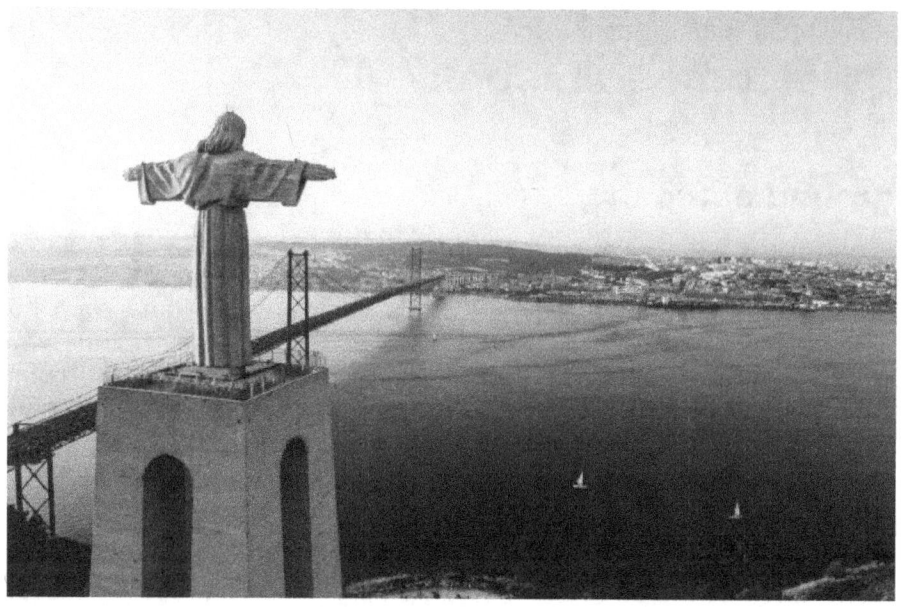

Traveling Around Lisbon

When you are preparing for a trip to a new country, a country that is unfamiliar to you, you need to ensure that you do your research and give yourself time to get to know more about the place you're traveling to. This means that you need to become accustomed to the places and landscape of your destination. Traveling around Lisbon should be fun and spark the adventurer inside of you.

Lisbon has so much to offer, but you need to know where to look. You also need to know what you are expecting from your Lisbon experience. Therefore, learning about the different areas, must-see places, local secrets, and tourist hotspots will help you choose what you do and do not want to do or see in Lisbon. You will not want to see every attraction, and you definitely do not need to in order to make your trip worthwhile. The best approach to traveling around Lisbon is to know what you want to get out of your trip and then where and how you can achieve your travel dreams. Below are some Lisbon travel tips to make your stay easier and much more fulfilling:

- Get a Lisboa Card, the city's tourist pass.
- Pre-book or book online beforehand.
- Find free tours like walking tours or places with no entrance fees.
- Carry cash on you, always.
- Keep your valuables on you and secure to prevent being pickpocketed.
- Use uber instead of public transport.

- Take tram 12 instead of tram 28.
- Wear comfortable shoes or pack walking shoes in your backpack.

Lisbon is very accommodating for tourists as it is the ultimate holiday destination and tourist hub of Portugal. You can jot down the must-see places and activities you would like to do and then work backwards by figuring out how you are going to do it and how you are going to get there. Lisbon's lines for many attractions are known to be long, so planning ahead and pre-booking are essential. You may even have to postpone certain activities due to the long lines. This is why remaining flexible yet organizing when traveling around a big city like Lisbon is the perfect combination for a fun-filled holiday abroad.

You may be a person who is looking for outdoor activities or you may want to enjoy the nightlife and unique café culture of a European city. No matter what kind of traveler you are, Lisbon can surprise you and can open your eyes to so many possibilities, as long as you are ready for it. Having some travel hacks under your belt is always helpful as well as some insight into the local travel systems and tourist traps you may experience.

Travel Tips

Things to Know Before You Arrive in Lisbon

Before you set off for Lisbon, you need to make sure you have an idea of where you are going and what you are going to do as well as how you are going to do it. While you could have a perfect plan in your head, this will not always become your reality once you arrive in Lisbon. The city has its own energy and its own rules, so you will need to adapt to it and learn how to go with the pace, the people, and the social as well as mandatory expectations of Lisbon.

Transport, accommodation, and money are essential when traveling. Therefore, you need to make sure you have these needs met, but how? Well, in Lisbon there are many modes of transport, but you also need to think about where you are staying and your budget, which both affect how you are going to travel around the city. For instance, people who are on a budget may opt for walking or sharing transport services or even look for promotion codes or discounts. This you can find on apps like Uber. Lisbon has decent public transport, but using trams to get around the busy streets of the city is not a smart choice. Some trams and public transport can actually end up being more expensive than using lift apps or just walking. Local taxis can also overcharge tourists, so making use of a travel card for trams or the metro with a set price, or using an app is your best option. Therefore, make sure to download transportation and even food delivery apps that are operational in Lisbon to make your life a little easier.

Getting by is quite hassle-free in Lisbon as it is an international hub. Therefore, speaking English to most people will not be a problem, but it is always useful to learn some Portuguese phrases that will help you connect with locals and find your way around the city when following directions or looking for hidden gems. You can learn a few Portuguese greetings and phrases before your trip or even on the plane to make sure you can get through any lost-in-translation situations.

Before you start exploring, you will need to invest in some good walking shoes because you *will* walk a lot! In addition to getting a travel card to get around, you will need to rely on your two feet when moving through the streets and neighborhoods of Lisbon. The city is old and some streets are narrow and best to experience by foot. Make sure to pack your most comfortable and reliable sneakers, your water bottle, and a fully charged phone or a map to navigate the city.

Lisbon is an international hub, so there is no need to worry about getting stuck anywhere. People are open and more than happy to help. As long as you have your essentials with you, including your passport, cash or credit card, comfortable footwear and clothes, an equipped backpack that are safely stored, then you are more than ready for your Lisbon adventures!

First-Time Traveler?

Lisbon is a unique city with its own rules, culture, and overall vibe, but there are some golden rules and tricks to traveling that all travelers need to follow. If you are a first-time traveler, below is a list of some tips and tricks to keep in mind before and during your trip:

- Make sure your passport is valid.
- If necessary, apply for a visa a few months before you plan to leave.
- Do your research on your destination, specifically the culture, history, and geography.
- Create a realistic budget with extra cash or savings for some unforeseen expenses.
- Take out travel insurance to cover certain things you would like to protect.
- Get your banking or credit card ready to have access to international use.
- Pack travel-friendly clothes and gear that is suitable for the season you will be traveling.
- Pack adaptors or purchase universal adaptors to charge your electronic devices.
- Pack your essential or chronic medication as well as emergency first-aid items to last you for more than your stay.
- Book some tours or transportation trips in advance and look for early bird and online specials.

- Have a secure backpack or small bag to keep your valuables on your person to avoid pickpockets.
- Try to assimilate and look a little less touristy to avoid being overcharged, falling victim to tourist traps, and being exploited in general. Try to remain informed and vigilant when exploring foreign places.

Look Out for Tourist Traps

In any tourist destination, you will be at risk of getting into tourist traps. Some people shrug it off while others detest the audacity of these traps. If you want to prevent yourself from falling into a tourist trap, you need to be aware of the specific traps you may find in Lisbon. Below is a list of some traps you should try to avoid:

- The tram 28 as a mode of transport.
- Long lines for the Santa Justa Elevator.
- Pricey entrance fees for replicas of ancient buildings.
- Rushed and overpriced guided tours.
- Trendy or popular bakeries and restaurants with common foods, think pastel de nata, with overpriced food you can get somewhere else.
- Tourist souvenir shops.
- Viewpoints from monuments or structures with entrance fees.

While these are only a few of the most common tourist traps, you may find yourself unaware of others. The best thing you can do is observe, do your research, and follow your gut. With a rough or well-planned itinerary, budget, and travel wishlist, you will be less vulnerable to tourist traps. Remember, your holiday is *yours* and you have the ability to make your Lisbon trip the best it can be for you!

Traveling on a Budget?

Of course, travel is a privilege, but you should not believe the lie that travel is only for the rich. In fact, Lisbon is a perfect place for travelers who are on a budget. You would still need to save up for your flight and accommodation, but even then, you can find discounts and a variety of options that fit within your travel budget. As a solo traveler or a family traveling abroad, there are definitely ways to avoid spending money or extra money while still enjoying the beauty of being on holiday in Lisbon.

We have compiled a list of some money-saving tricks to help you be more savvy when it comes to spending money and living life as a tourist, as being a tourist in any city can always have you end up spending more than you usually would on an average day at home. Below are some tips and tricks to saving money during your Lisbon adventure:

- Buy a Lisboa Card to get entrance into top attractions as well as unlimited rides on public transportation, including the tram, bus, and metro, even the elevators and funiculars.
- Pre-book certain tours and even your accommodation in advance to avoid higher prices, or book during the off-season.
- Take a ride on tram 28 after getting your Lisboa Card to view some must-see spots, buildings, and streets.
- Visit free sites and do free activities, which could be a picnic in the park, a day at the beach, and viewpoints also known as *miradouros*.
- Buy groceries at local markets or grocery stores and plan daily meals instead of eating out or relying on takeout.
- Walk the city and spend time roaming the streets of Alfama, Baixa, Bairro Alto, and other historic districts to admire the local street art and architecture.
- Book certain tours online or via apps to get promo codes or online discounts.
- Visit Museu Berardo on Saturdays for free entrance or by using a Lisboa Card for a discount on your entrance fee.
- Avoid ordering drinks at restaurants and rather carry your own bottle of water as you explore the city.
- Avoid accepting bread when sitting down at a restaurant as this appetizer is an additional cost and not free.
- Spend a relaxing day at a local park or garden, specifically the Jardim de Estrela or the Estua Fria on Sundays for free entry.
- Give yourself a reasonable daily allowance to avoid overspending or impulsive purchases.
- Eat where the locals eat to avoid overpriced meals at tourist hotspots.
- Take a free train ride to Sintra and Cascais with your Lisboa Card, and spend the day roaming the old towns or at one of the nearby beaches.

Create Your Own Itinerary

A holiday should never feel like a job or become a reason for lingering stress. Instead, we all deserve a holiday that is stress-free and filled with joy, ease, and some room for spontaneity. A smart way to approach your holiday is by being prepared and creating your own itinerary that serves your needs and travel dreams. When trying to create an itinerary, you need to consider

- Your ideal destination
- The length of your stay
- The reason for your visit

- Your budget
- People who you are traveling with
- Your unique interests

Once you have a clear idea about these factors, you can start to create a template or a rough draft of your itinerary. You should also remember that nothing is set in stone, especially when it comes to international travel. There will always be the potential for unforeseen events, setbacks, delays, and changes or adjustments. Therefore, seeing your itinerary as partially complete throughout your planning and actual trip is a wise approach to traveling. Being flexible is a must when you are on holiday as people are people and we can change our minds or make impulsive decisions, we can also be faced with external and uncontrollable factors.

Creating an itinerary can involve creating a calendar, a timetable, a list (extensive or vague), or even notes jotted down on your phone. Whichever format works for you will be the best way to go forward in your preparation. Doing your research beforehand is a must as well as knowing what *you* want out of the trip. You need to be able to adapt your itinerary to serve your needs while also ensuring that you are realistic about what you can, cannot, and want to do. Below are some tips you can follow when you are busy creating an itinerary that is perfect for you and your Lisbon getaway:

- Do your research, and make use of the internet to answer all your pre-trip questions that may concern you as well as general topics like cost of living, routes and regions, transport and laws, etc.
- Create your travel wishlist with all your must-see attractions and activities. You can structure this list in order of importance; from musts to would likes, maybes and alternative or spontaneous options.
- Create a rough calendar or list based on the dates and length of your travel.
- Give yourself a realistic budget for each day or for the entire length of your trip.
- Ask local contacts or friends for advice, their travel hacks, and personal experiences concerning accommodation, transport, and activities.
- Pencil in your to-do list and any additions into your rough itinerary before finishing it up and leaving for Lisbon!

Your itinerary could look like the template below which you can use and adapt for your Lisbon trip:

Week 1

Day 1	*Must-do activity: Cost: +- Additional/Alternative activity:*
Day 2	*Must-do activity: Cost: +- Additional/Alternative activity:*
Day 3	*Must-do activity: Cost: +- Additional/Alternative activity:*

Day 4	Must-do activity: Cost: +- Additional/Alternative activity:
Day 5	Must-do activity: Cost: +- Additional/Alternative activity:
Day 6	Must-do activity: Cost: +- Additional/Alternative activity:
Day 7	Must-do activity: Cost: +- Additional/Alternative activity:

Week 2

Day 1	Must-do activity: Cost: +- Additional/Alternative activity:
Day 2	Must-do activity: Cost: +- Additional/Alternative activity:
Day 3	Must-do activity: Cost: +- Additional/Alternative activity:
Day 4	Must-do activity: Cost: +- Additional/Alternative activity:
Day 5	Must-do activity: Cost: +- Additional/Alternative activity:
Day 6	Must-do activity: Cost: +- Additional/Alternative activity:
Day 7	Must-do activity: Cost: +- Additional/Alternative activity:

Chapter 2: Enjoy Lisbon Throughout the Year

Annual Festivals and Events

January

- Epiphany: On January 6th, this event occurs as a celebration of the arrival of the Three Kings to mark the end of Christmas and is usually celebrated in rural towns as they sing traditional carols. People come together to eat a traditional meal, similar to a Christmas meal with the addition of *bolo rei* also known as king cake.

February

- Carnival: This traditional festival occurs at the end of every winter, where people dress in costumes and parade the streets along with music, dance, beer, and traditional Portuguese food.

March

- *Meia Maratona de Lisboa*, the Lisbon Half Marathon: This marathon takes place over the Tejo River, moves through the city and then finishes at the Jerónimos Monastery.

April

- Indie Lisboa: An 11-day independent film festival that holds screenings of experimental and short films as well as documentaries with people of the industries debating and engaging with the works.
- Peixe em Lisboa: Also known as the Fish in Lisbon, is an annual seafood festival with food prepared by some of the best Portuguese and international chefs at the Eduardo VII Park.
- April 25th, *Dia da Liberdade*, Freedom Day: A national holiday that is observed to commemorate the liberation of the Portuguese people as they revolted against the dictatorship during the 1970s.

May

- Lisbon Book Fair: This book fair occurs between May and June. It is held at Eduardo Vil Park where literature lovers gather to purchase books of all sorts and in all languages.
- Santos Populares, The Month of Patron Saints: Is a time when people celebrate the saints of Portugal with dances, music, and food and beverages in the streets. There are many festivals and street parties held throughout the month of June.
- On June 12th, The Feast of Saint Anthony Parade is held. People dance in the streets with the traditional meal being grilled sardines with wine or sangria.

July

- Delta Tejo: A musical festival held in Alto da Ajuda, where live ethnic and traditional music is performed, including Portuguese, Cape Verdean, and Brazilian music.
- Sumol Summer Fest: A popular music festival that takes place at the Ericeira resort. The festival includes electronic music, house, hip hop, and reggae and is a perfect party to start off the summer as it is held along the beach. People can also participate in watersports while enjoying the music through to the night until the next morning.

August

- Jazz em Agosto: Is a jazz event that is hosted at the open-air amphitheater of the Fundação Calouste Gulbenkian, welcoming the beginning of summer. The concerts offer jazz music from international artists.
- Festival dos Oceanos: Is a two-week event that displays the local artists of Lisbon. There are exhibitions, shows, street performances, and live music concerts across the city in different neighborhoods, including Belém and Parque das Nações.

September

- Santa Casa Alfama Festival: A musical festival dedicated to the traditional Portuguese fado music. The event is held in the historic neighborhood which is perfect as the music, dating back to the 1800s, is an integral part of Portuguese music culture and social life.

October

- October, the Lisbon Marathon starts in Cascais at the Praça do Comércio and is 26 miles long. Runners get to race along the city's waterfront and spectators can also watch the race. There are different routes and different distances, including the shorter Luso Half Marathon and the Vodafone 10K marathon.

November

- Lisbon and Sintra Film Festival: People in the film industry come together to celebrate and appreciate the art form.

December

- Christmas: Avenida da Liberdade and other streets and squares in Baixa and Chiado are decorated with all things Christmas to celebrate the birth of Jesus Christ. The many Christmas lights make these areas of the city magical and ready for the festive season.
- New Year's Eve: People gather to welcome the new year along the river in Praça do Comércio and Parque das Nações. There is a fireworks display, live music and many DJs that make this event memorable.

Activities to Do For Each Season

Summer

- Spending the day swimming or sunbathing on the many stunning beaches around Cascais or just outside of the city.
- Alfresco dining on warm summer nights are perfect in districts such as Alfama, Calçada do Duque, Bairro Alto, or in Bonjardim.
- Celebrate summer by attending festivals, for example, Festival dos Oceanos, Baixo Anima, Festas dos Santos Populares, and Feast of Saint Anthony.
- Go for a picnic with some delicious food bought at Mercado da Ribeira, Conserveira de Lisboa, or Manuel Tavares.
- Spend your summer evenings out at a Ginjinha, Noobai Café, Portas Largas, or Doca de Alcântara.
- Take day trips out of the city and spend the whole day outside in nature, around the special town of Sintra, as well as the Pena Palace, Setúbal, Sado, or Avenida Luísa Todi.

Fall

- Visit the Calouste Gulbenkian Museum.
- Take a ride on Tram 28 to spot the many attractions of the city.
- Enjoy the view from Lisbon's viewpoints like the elevator of the Santa Justa Lift.
- Visit the Alfama District to discover some trendy cafés.
- Wander around the market of Feira da Ladra.
- Spend hours having a fun night out in and around the district of Bairro Alto.

Winter

- Go to a Fado house and watch a performance.

- Shop at the Christmas Markets, including Campo Pequeno, Wonderland Parque Eduardo VII, Natalis.
- Spend New Year's Eve in the Praça de Comércio
- Go on a foodie crawl to taste traditional Portuguese food -Cabo Verde.
- Go on a wine tour.
- Enjoy admiring the many traditional *miradouros*, for example, Miradouro das Portas do Sol, Miradouro da Graça, Miradouro de São Pedro de Alcântara, and Miradouro da Nossa Senhora do Monte.
- Spend an educational afternoon inside one of the many museums of the city, namely the National Museum of Natural History and Science, the National Museum Of Ancient Art, The Maritime Museum, The Fado Museum, the museum at the Luz Stadium, and the National Tile Museum.

Spring

- Spend time soaking up the fresh spring air along the Tagus River in Belém.
- Go to a music festival to welcome the warm weather like the Rock in Rio Festival.
- Take an opportunity to eat al fresco.
- Go on a hiking trail in Sintra, Cascais, or Cabo de Roca.
- Spend time under sunnier skies by taking a ride on one of the Gondolas while enjoying ice cream at Parque das Nações.
- Visit the Monserrate Palace.
- Take a trip to the Cristo-Rei to admire the statue and take some great photographs.
- Challenge yourself and take a bike ride around the hilly city.
- Spend time at markets or book fairs, like the Feira do Livro.

- Go to the Out Jazz event.
- Pack a picnic basket and enjoy lunch at one of the local parks or gardens, specifically the Botanical Gardens- Jardim Botânico d'Ajuda.

Chapter 3: Top Sights, Streets, and Secrets of the City

Must-See Attractions

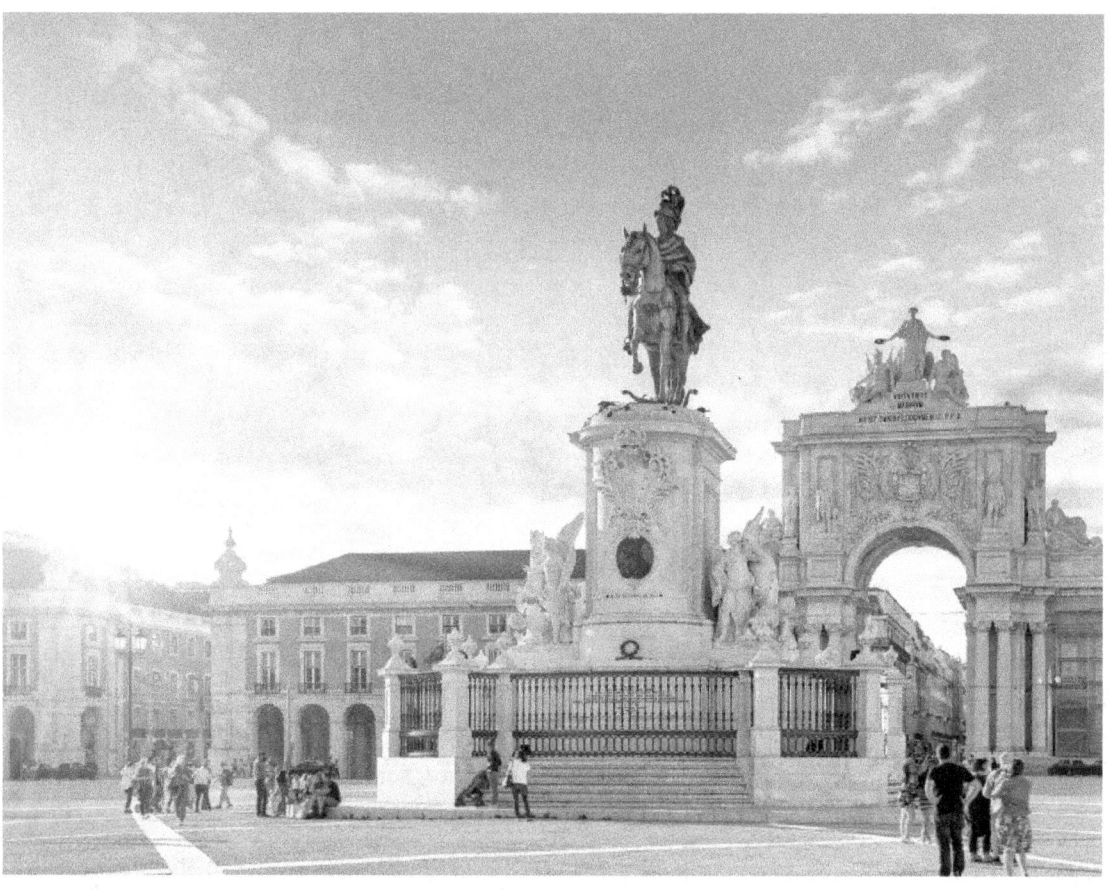

Lisbon is undeniably a tourist hotspot with many attractions that draw tourists to marvel at the architecture, historical sites, and art that makes the city stand out among other European cities and towns. There are a few must-see attractions that one just cannot leave out of their travel wishlists. When in Lisbon, you will just need to visit some of these attractions:

- *Castelo de São Jorge*: The São Jorge Castle is a medieval castle located in the historic center of the city, Santa Maria Maior. The castle was built by Visigoths in the fifth century with the purpose of being a fortress. Then, in the 11th century, the Moors expanded the fortress, making it larger in size. In the 12th century, with the reign of Alfonso I, the building went through renovations to serve as an official Royal Palace. In 1938, with Salazar in power, the palace was restored to symbolize the patriotism of Portugal. The history of the castle is fascinating and can be seen by its construction as well as its external and internal features. The castle is now a historical monument for locals and tourists to admire. It is open every day of the week from 9:00 am to 9:00 pm. A single ticket for an adult costs €10, and this covers your admission as well as a guided tour.
- *Palácio da Ajuda*: The Palace of Ajuda is a monument that was initially built for the royal family. Its construction took decades as there were many issues with the actual build as well as external political issues, including it being invaded by Napoleon in 1807. The palace was completed in the 19th century and finally became the permanent residence of the royal family of Portugal when King Luis I was king. The royal family was forced to move out of the palace and go into exile during the republican revolution in 1910. The construction and interior of the palace have been preserved, and the palace is now open to the public for daily visits. The entrance fee costs €5.

- The Berardo Museum of Modern and Contemporary Art: this art museum holds iconic works from artists including Warhol, Picasso, Dali, and Pollock. For art lovers, this museum is paradise. There are permanent and temporary exhibits that are held in the Berardo and all exhibits are showcased to have visitors admire the different modern movements as well as the experimental spirit of contemporary art. The admission fee for the Berardo Museum is €5.
- *Elevador de Santa Justa* or *Elevador do Carmo:* Santa Justa Lift is a great way to view Lisbon's skyline and get breathtaking views of the city. The elevator is not new, in fact, its construction was completed in 1902, designed by architect Raoul Mesnier du Ponsard. The lift actually shares similar features as that of the Eiffel Tower in Paris, as du Ponsard was a student of the man who built the Eiffel Tower. Initially, the purpose of the lift was to connect the lower streets of Baixa to Carmo Square. This function was used and was convenient for locals, but today the lift serves as a tourist attraction as many people flock from all over the world to marvel at the views the lift provides. You will also find a restaurant on the top floor of the building, perfect for visitors to sit down and take in the skyline of the city. It costs €5.30 for a ride, but is free with a Lisboa Card as it is part of the city tourist pass.
- *Sé-Lisbon Cathedral*: This cathedral of Lisbon is located in the Baixa district and is the oldest church in the city. It was built in 1147 and has gone through many renovations over the centuries due to the earthquake of 1775 as well as political movements and changes in rulers throughout Portuguese history. The architecture resembles the many periods and tests the cathedral stood through. The cathedral's main chapel showcases the neoclassical and Rococo styles. The history

and stories that the cathedral holds are astounding, with King Afonso IV buried in the cathedral. The monument is a national treasure and is free to visit for all who are interested in Lisbon's history and its marvelous architecture.
- *Praça do Comércio*: Commerce Square is a hub for tourists and locals alike. The square is the largest and most popular in the city. Located right where the former royal palace stood along the riverfront, the square is a place where people gather to shop, people-watch, and browse around to get in the energy of the city of Lisbon.
- *Museu Nacional de Arte Antiga*: This art museum is located in the municipality of Lapa and holds stunning artworks from across the world. The building itself is a unique shade of yellow, lemon-colored and dates back to the 17th century. The palace now showcases Lisbon's architecture from the outside and its appreciation for art on the inside. There are many historical pieces in the museum, including the ceremonial armchair of King Afonso V. You can also find some souvenirs from Vasco da Gama's explorations as well as Asian and European paintings. The museum is open to the public from 10:00 am to 6:00 pm on Tuesdays to Sundays. The entrance fee is priced from €6 to €10 depending on the exhibition package you choose.
- *Mosteiro dos Jerónimos*: Jerónimos Monastery is located in Belém and is an example of the Portuguese Gothic Manueline architecture style. The construction of the former monastery started in 1501 as it was a symbol to celebrate Portuguese explorer Vasco da Gama's return. Despite construction beginning in the 14th century, the monastery was only completed in the 17th century. Today, the tomb of Vasco da Gama resides in the Jerónimos Monastery. After the

secularization of the monastery in 1833, it now serves as a national heritage site. The monastery became a UNESCO World Heritage Site in 1983. You can visit the church for free and the entrance fee for the monastery is €10.
- *Torre de Belém:* The Belém Tower is a must-see attraction due to its location and unique design. The tower was built in the 150os and follows a Manuelino architectural style. The tower was built to serve as a defense construction as well as an area of embarkation for many Portuguese explorers. Due to its initial purpose, it is now viewed as a symbol of Portugal's Age of Discoveries and is a World Heritage Site. The admission fee is €6 for adults and this includes a guided tour as well as permission to roam the tower and its rooftop terrace with views of the Tagus River.

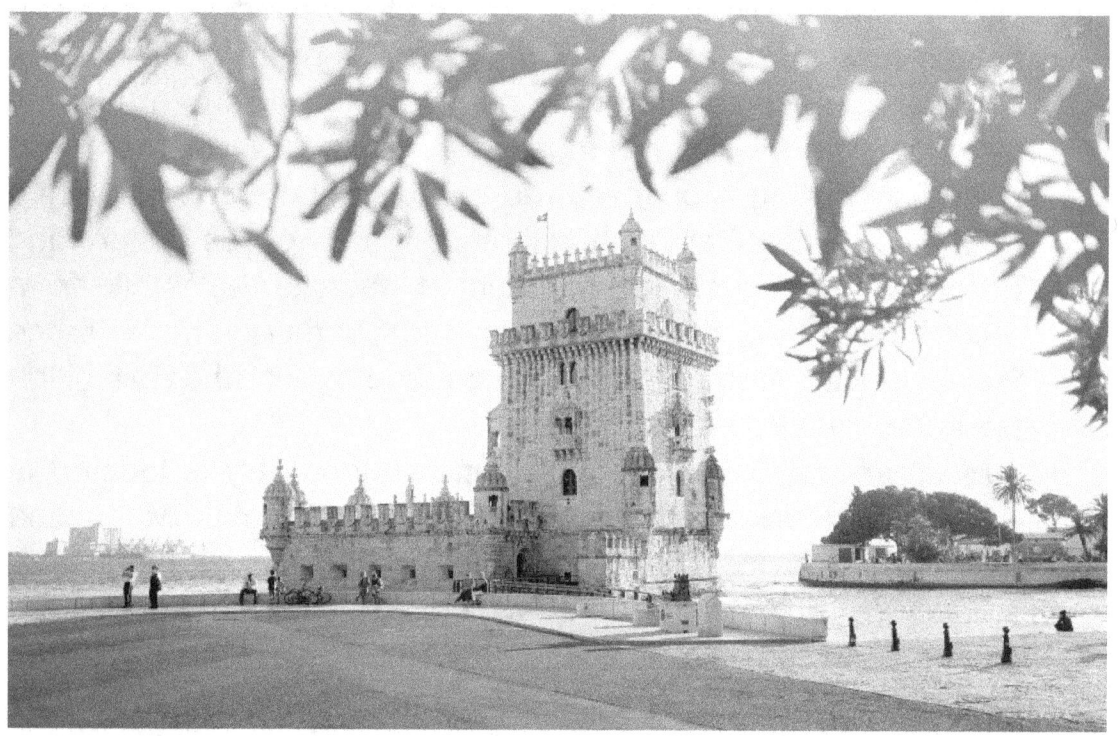

- *Padrão dos Descobrimentos*: Monument of the Discoveries is within walking distance from the Belém Tower. While some disagree on the prestige and acclaim of this monument, it still showcases the architecture of its glory days during Portuguese colonialism and the dictatorship at the time. Standing at 52m, the building was first made from perishable materials and was then reconstructed in 1960 to make an official monument to commemorate the death of Henry the Navigator.
- *Museu Calouste Gulbenkian-Coleção do Fundador*: The Founder's Collection at Museu Calouste Gulbenkian includes art from Western and Eastern backgrounds. You can find rare Egyptian treasures on display as well as Impressionist paintings. The art is diverse but precious with old-world artifacts including mummy masks, porcelain objects, and an exquisite collection of jewelry, while you can also admire masterpieces by Rembrandt and sculptor Rodin. You can visit the Calouste Gulbenkian to see these amazing works of art from Wednesday to Monday, from 10:00 am to 6:00 pm. The combo ticket that includes both the Coleção Moderna and the Coleção do Fundador is priced at €10.

The Stunning Streets of Lisbon

You can take a walk through the many cobbled and hilly streets of Lisbon, or you can take a ride on the classic tram 28E. If you choose the latter, your ride will be an old-fashioned yellow city tram. Taking time to view the city's charm is a must when you are in Lisbon. Just looking out from the tram ride or taking a stroll in the late afternoon to watch the city come to life as the sunsets and the nightlife is on display. Below is a list of some unique and iconic streets you can explore in Lisbon:

- Avenida da Liberdade: This is one of the main streets of Lisbon, connecting Praça dos Restauradores and Praça do Marquês de Pombal. Walking down this street will allow you to admire authentic Portuguese architecture dating back to the 19th century. There are squares with fountains and statues that make this street even more charming. The avenue is central

and also abundant in attractions as it showcases the architecture of Lisbon's interesting and eclectic history, with these old buildings contrasted with contemporary fashion stores.
- Rua Augusta: This is a central and popular pedestrian street in Lisbon and it is filled with people walking up and down to take in the charm of this part of the city. There are cafés and shops along the street and the buildings are colorful with stunning terraces and mosaic tiles. Portuguese architecture and lively culture are displayed along this street. From this street, you can also spot the Arco da Rua Augusta.
- Rua Cor de Rosa: Also known as Rua Nova do Carvalho, this iconic pink street is always photo-ready and Instagram-worthy. Not only does the aesthetic of the street catch your eye, but the street is lined with trendy cafés and bars that you can enjoy for a tasty meal or a night of drinking and socializing.
- Calçada do Duque: This street allows you to view the São Jorge Castle and cityscape of Lisbon. There are also great eateries along this street where you can enjoy some traditional dishes before continuing your walk, viewing the precious architecture of Lisbon.
- Rua do Carmo: Due to its location, this street is always busy and full of life. The street is connected to popular neighborhoods like Baixa and Bairro Alto, therefore, you will find many locals and tourists along this street. The street is vibrant and showcases the life and everyday energy of Lisbon. You can take a walk down this street to observe the people of Lisbon, and walk a little further to reach the popular attraction, Elevador de Santa Justa.
- Rua do Sacramento à Lapa: Found in Estrela, you can take a stroll down this street and take in the feeling of the Portugal

that existed decades ago. Here, you can find the many romantic mansions, grand embassies, and Neo-Manueline constructions in all their glory. The many buildings situated along this street are on display for you to take in the history of the country and the design of the city.

- Rua da Bica: This is one of the most iconic and most photographed streets in Lisbon. The entire street screams "classic Portugal." From the colorful houses with their balconies to the yellow tram, this street is a must-see. As you walk down, you will be able to feel the true energy of the city and admire all its history. The street is found on many postcards, brochures, and travel advertisements of Lisbon, and naturally attracts so many tourists each day.
- Rua do Vale: This is a street that should not be overlooked. It holds so much history, with its traditional Portuguese pavement it leads you on a path to the Church of Nossa Senhora das Mercês as well as many displays of hidden gems full of art and design, including the Atelier-Museu Júlio Pomar. You can also continue to walk down this street until you reach the São Bento Palace.
- Calçada de Santana: This sidewalk is located in the heart of Lisbon and reveals its age with grace. It is narrow, steep, and lined with colorful old buildings as well as offering a view of the Tagus River. This narrow street is conveniently located and connects you to other places of interest. As you make your way down, you can view the old church Igreja da Pen, and you can also take a detour to reach the Santos courtyard via Rua Martim Vaz.
- Rua dos Remédios: Located in Alfama, this street is home to some great traditional Fado houses where you can enjoy a

quick meal. The street also has preserved Manueline portals and stunning tiles dating back to the 18th century.

Learn About Local Treasures

Fado Houses

Known as *Casas de Fado*, these eateries are popular places for locals and tourists to sit and enjoy traditional Portuguese meals while watching live fado music. The fado music is integrated into Portuguese culture, specifically among the working class, due to its origins stemming from sailors who experienced hardships and difficult working conditions during the 19th century. While the music may be melancholic and mournful, it serves as a great background music for a relaxing time out in a fado house, surrounded by aromas of Portuguese food, the sounds of the language and traditional harmonies. There are many fado houses and some are more expensive than others, but they offer a unique experience that you will not be able to find anywhere else. You will get a meal and a show when you go to one of these houses. While meals can start at €30, which can be pricey, you will also be entertained with live music and local artists without any extra charge. To avoid going to expensive, more tourist-friendly fado houses, you can ask locals about their favorite houses and go there instead. A popular fado house is Fado in Chiado, another beloved fado house is Parreirinha in Alfama.

A Day Trip to Sintra

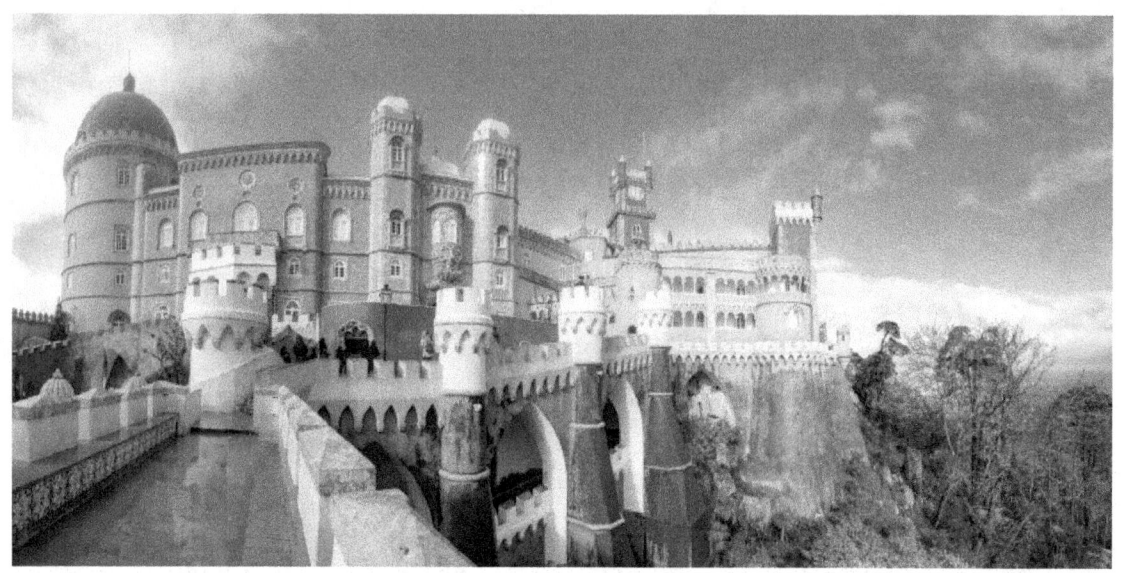

A visit to this historic town is a must! The medieval architecture has preserved this town's history, and walking through the narrow streets in Sintra will make you feel like you have traveled back in time. The town is a UNESCO World Heritage Site for so many reasons. The town holds palaces where royals used to reside in and it is also home to the Castle of the Moors, which was built in the 8th and 9th centuries. The entire atmosphere of the place holds romantic streets, buildings, and gardens. The Palácio Nacional da Pena is located in Sintra and the entrance costs about €15. To get to Sintra from Lisbon, you can travel by car as the town is only a 30-minute drive away from Lisbon city, or you can take the train from Oriente station and the travel time from the station to Sintra is about 45 minutes. While it may be 15 minutes extra travel time, the fare will cost you around €2, while ordering a cab or Uber will cost anywhere from €20 to €30. Be prepared to walk the old roads of this town by bringing a water bottle and your best walking shoes. If you get hungry, you can always sit down at one of the lovely traditional restaurants for lunch. Spending a day in Sintra is worth it as it is not far from central Lisbon, and this day trip offers you an opportunity to discover the treasures of an old Portuguese town that still stands today, revealing the perseverance of the country's people.

Explore Alfama

This hilly district of Lisbon is known for its Visigothic influence as well as its Moorish architecture. This area is a real gem that you can find in Lisbon. Alfama shows off the traditional side of Lisbon, with its narrow streets and small local cafés. The area is still inhabited by locals, so when you walk through the cobblestoned streets of this district you will get a close-community feeling that you cannot experience in other parts of the city. You can also observe the everyday Portuguese laidback lifestyle as locals socialize and sell their produce. Alfama is really a great way to get to know Portuguese culture without reading a history book or taking a guided tour. Here you will just feel and observe, and become part of the community.

LX Factory

This is a cultural and creative hub of the city. Located in Lapa, this warehouse square is where locals and tourists can gather and watch live concerts, fashion shows, film screenings, and admire art exhibitions. There are also stalls with locals selling their products, trendy cafés, as well as vibey restaurants. This is an area dedicated to innovation and artistic expression. While most of Lisbon is dominated by old buildings holding old-world charm and art works from past centuries, LX Factory showcases newer work from up and coming artists with different artistic mediums. If you are looking for an evening of entertainment and inspiration with a tasty meal and cold beer, you can visit LX Factory for all that.

Chapter 4: Taste the Flavors of the City

Dining Out

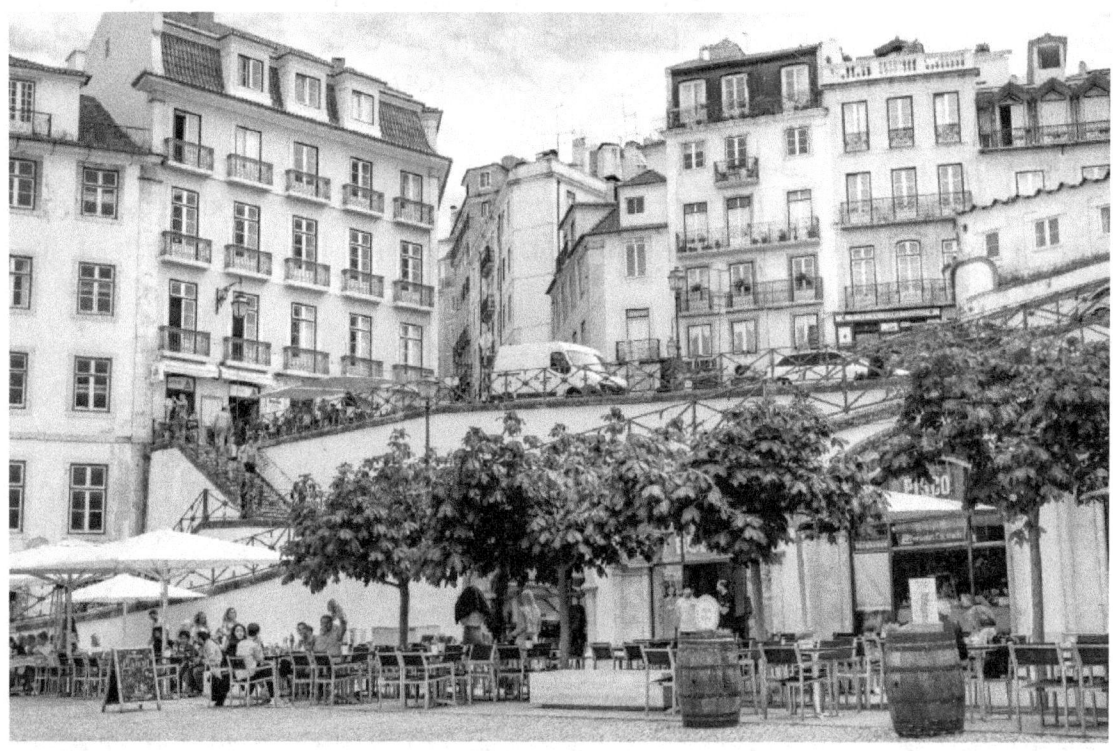

Top Restaurants in the City

Below is a list of the best restaurants in the city, beginning with fine dining establishments to moderately priced comfort food:

- Sala—*Cuisine*: Mediterranean, European, Healthy; *Location*: Rua dos Bacalhoeiros 103
- ALMA Henrique Sá Pessoa—*Cuisine*: Mediterranean, European, Contemporary; *Location*: Rua Anchieta 15 Chiado
- Belcanto—*Cuisine*: Contemporary, Portuguese, Vegetarian Friendly; *Location*: Rua Serpa Pinto 10A
- Feitoria Restaurant & Wine Bar—*Cuisine*: International, Mediterranean, European; *Location*: Doca do Bom Sucesso Altis Belém Hotel & Spa
- Versículo do Faia—Cuisine: Seafood, Mediterranean; *Location*: Rua da Barroca 60A Bairro Alto
- Augusto Lisboa—*Cuisine*: European, Healthy, Portuguese; *Location*: Rua Santa Marinha, 26
- Re'Tasco—*Cuisine*: International, European, Grill; *Location*: Estrada do Calhariz de Benfica 13
- Grau Douro Tapas & Wine Bar—*Cuisine*: Portuguese, Contemporary, Bar; *Location*: Rua Duques de Bragança 5M
- Seventh Brunch Coffee—*Cuisine*: Café, European; *Location*: Calçada do Combro 147 Chiado
- EstaminÉ Art Food Drink—*Cuisine*: Contemporary, Healthy, Bar; *Location*: Calçado do Monte 86 A Graça

Popular Bars

Below is a list of some popular bars that the people of Lisbon, visitors and locals alike, have enjoyed:

- Delirium Cafe Lisboa—*Cuisine*: Brew Pub, Bar, European; *Location*: Calçada Nova de São Francisco 2A
- Jam Club—*Cuisine*: Bar, Portuguese; *Location*: Travessa dos Inglesinhos 49

- The Beer Station—*Cuisine*: Bar, Pub; *Location*: Largo Duque do Cadaval 17
- Cerveja Canil—*Cuisine*: Brew Bar, International, Pub; *Location*: Rua dos Douradores 133

Eating Like a Local

Lisbon is a foodie's dream, with restaurants and eateries offering different cuisines at varying prices. The city has food for everyone, and depending on your food preferences and dietary needs, Lisbon will have you spoiled for choice when it comes to eating out. You can find a great bistro with local meals or a high-end restaurant with quality sushi or even a delicious Italian pizza. If you are looking forward to trying out the many local dishes of Portugal, then you need to try out some of these in the list below:

- Pork sandwich, *bifana*
- Beef sandwich, *prego*
- Green soup, *caldo verde*
- Salted cod, *bacalhau*
- Meat stew, *cozido à portuguesa*
- Sardines, *sardinhas*
- Piri-piri chicken, *frango de churrasco piri-piri*
- Custard tart, *pastéis de nata*
- Rice pudding, *arroz doce*
- Portuguese biscuit cake, *bolo de bolacha*
- Fortified liqueur wine of Porto, *port*

Local Delis, Markets, and Kitchens

- Floresta Das Escadinhas—*Cuisine*: Mediterranean, Barbecue, European; *Location*: Rua de Santa Justa 3
- STŌ Mercearia—*Cuisine*: Mediterranean, Contemporary, Portuguese; *Location*: Rua dos Fanqueiros 85 Santa Maria Maior
- Erva Príncipe—*Cuisine*: Café, Mediterranean, European; *Location*: Largo da Paz, nr 1A–Ajuda
- Donna Taca, Art & Wine Bar—*Cuisine*: International, European, Deli; *Location*: Rua do Telhal 4B
- Ao 26 Vegan Food Project—*Cuisine*: European, Healthy, Portuguese; *Location:* Rua Vítor Cordon 26

Culinary Experiences

Unique Dining and Culinary Activities

These dining and culinary experiences can be done as part of a self-guided tour or you can book a guided tour with a local tour guide or tourism company. Below we will look at some unique dining experiences that Lisbon has to offer.

Lisbon at Night: Fado Show and Dinner

The traditional dining and show experience at a fado house has been recognized as folk heritage by UNESCO, which means you have not really experienced Portuguese dining without dining out at a fado house. The idea is to have a traditional Portuguese meal while you watch a live performance by musicians playing traditional fado music. There are many fado houses in the city, but if you want to feel the comfort and richness of this tradition, you could look for popular fado houses that locals go to or houses in areas that are known for their dining and nightlife. Going to a fado house in a historic area like the Alfama district is also a good decision if you want to be immersed in Portuguese folk music and dining.

Wine Tasting in the Setúbal Wine Region

Taking a trip out of Lisbon to one of the wine regions of Portugal will make for an interesting, informative, and fun day out. You can either book a tour that includes transport or you can drive to Setúbal in a rental car and do a wine tasting experience or choose to try out a specific wine pairing. It is wise to book before the time if you want to do a wine tasting and get a tour and guide through the wine making process. Another option is to spend time roaming around the wine farms, or sit down to enjoy the local wine with a cheese board made up of local cheese and other snacks as you enjoy the calming vineyards. You can also follow the wine route and stop at different wine farms along your drive through Setúbal, including Quinta de Alcube and one of the oldest wineries, José Maria da Fonseca.

A Food Tour in Campo de Ourique

To get a more local experience of the food culture in Lisbon, you can take a stroll through Campo de Ourique. Taking the tram is a good idea, or if you are willing to walk around the streets of this trendy neighborhood, you are free to do so. You can wander through the food market, and restaurants, and indulge in some Portuguese baked goods. There are also great bars here that serve great wine and craft beer. This culinary adventure is an active foodie's dream. If you are willing to go on a physical journey through this part of town to discover delicious treats, then this is a good late afternoon-evening outing.

Pastéis de Nata Cooking Class

The famous creamy, custard pastry that is enjoyed by so many across the globe, are the *pastéis de nata* or known as a *pastel de nata*. This is a dessert that can be enjoyed any time of the day, with its perfect taste and texture it is easy to want more than one. So, how does this tasty treat come into being? You can learn how to make pastéis de nata by taking a cooking class with a professional chef. There are many cooking classes to choose from, and some offer a class dedicated to learning how to make the perfect pastéis de nata the traditional way. Classes range in price, but cost around €40 per person. Classes are usually taught in small groups and each person has the opportunity to make their own batch of these baked treats and of course enjoy them after the class.

Brunch and a Live Drag Show

The Portuguese love dinner and a show, so why not make your dining experience even more interesting by being served brunch and then watch a spectacular drag show. This special dining experience involves being served by drag chefs and enjoying a fantastic brunch buffet. You will be greeted by a host, and served a delicious meal, and then the fun will begin with a live drag show. You can enjoy your bottomless mimosas as you sing along and laugh with the audience and your entertainers. This experience requires you to make a booking beforehand. Tickets cost €42 and the event is held at the LX Factory at 11:00 am.

Shop at Mercado de Arroios

Another unique Portuguese food experience is shopping for fresh local produce at a Lisbon food market. You can walk through the many stalls at Lisbon's Mercado de Arroios. You can shop for local bread, cheese, vegetables, and other specialities. You can also take groceries and enjoy a picnic at a local park or take them home and try out a traditional Portuguese meal with the authentic ingredients you have picked out. This is an immersive culinary experience as you will be shopping like a local, becoming part of the Lisbon food culture. You can also try out some Portuguese phrases while buying food from local vendors, which is another way to become fully part of the community.

Introductory Portuguese Gastronomy Class

You can get to know how traditional Portuguese food is made by making your own meal in an introductory cooking class. There are many options when it comes to group cooking classes, so you can pick which class you would like to go to depending on the meals you will cook and the skills you will learn. Cooking classes are a fun way to learn new culinary skills as well as learn more about the Portuguese culture while meeting new people. Some classes involve cooking a three-course Portuguese meal with local ingredients, taught by a local chef. You can ask around or look for classes you are interested in. You could look for classes that involve learning specific skills or a certain dish. Other classes are more social and involve many different meals and a group dinner with wine after the class. The cost of a cooking class can range from €40 to €80 per person. Hosts are usually local chefs or guides who have experience in cooking traditional meals and teaching foreigners, so there is no need to worry about language barriers. Cooking classes are one of the many examples of how you can make memories and share special moments with locals and travelers, different people from all over the world, connecting over a good hearty meal and a bottle of Port!

Chapter 5: Where to Stay and Settle

Holiday Accommodations

Tourist-Friendly Accommodations

- TURIM Boulevard Hotel—*Location*: Avenida da Liberdade 159, Santo Antonio; *Price per night*: €617.38
- EPIC SANA Marquês Hotel—*Location*: Av. Fontes Pereira de Melo 8, Santo Antônio; *Price per night*: €323.49
- Pestana Palace Lisboa Hotel & National Monument—*Location*: Rua Jau 54, Alcântara; *Price per night*: €385.24
- Wine & Books Lisboa Hotel—*Location*: 56 Travessa da Memória, Ajuda; *Price per night*: €253.54
- Hotel Dom Carlos Park—*Location*: Av. Duque de Loulé 121, Santo Antonio; *Price per night*: €191.91
- Hotel Dom Carlos Liberty—*Location*: Rua Alexandre Herculano 13, Santo Antonio; *Price per night*: €191.91
- Lisboa Prata Boutique Hotel—*Location*: Rua da Prata 116, Santa Maria Maior; *Price per night*: €125.94
- Esquina Cosmopolitan Lodge—*Location*: Rua da Madalena 195, Santa Maria Maior; *Price per night*: €195.95
- Browns Downtown Hotel—*Location*: Rua Dos Sapateiros 69-79, Santa Maria Maior; *Price per night*: €170.93
- Discovery Apartment Estrela—*Location*: Rua de São Ciro 14 R/C, Estrela; *Price per night*: €223.94

- Martinhal Lisbon Chiado—*Location*: Rua das Flores 44, Chiado/Baixa, Misericórdia; *Price per night*: €336.44
- TURIM Europa Hotel—*Location*: Rua São Sebastião da Pedreira 19, Avenidas Novas; *Price per night*: €103.23

Budget Accommodations

- TURIM Alameda Hotel—*Location*: Av. Rovisco Pais 34, Arroios; *Price per night*: €94.02
- Rossio Hostel—*Location*: Calçada do Carmo 6- 2 dto, Santa Maria Maior; *Price per night*: €35.90
- Bluesock Hostels Lisboa—*Location*: 1 Rua Manuel Jesus Coelho, Santo Antonio; *Price per night*: €136.46
- HI Lisboa-Pousada de Juventude—*Location*: Rua Andrade Corvo 46, Avenidas Novas; *Price per night*: €55.81
- Avenue Rooms & Suites—*Location*: Rua Rodrigues Sampaio 138, Santo Antonio; *Price per night*: €61.99
- Lisb'on Hostel—*Location*: Rua Do Ataide 7A, Misericordia; *Price per night*: €26.98
- Rodamón Lisboa—*Location*: Rua dos Fanqueiros 300, Santa Maria Maior; *Price per night*: €47.43

Rural and Local Homestays

- Quinta das Pedras—*Location*: EN 117 Quinta das Pedras, 2605-213, Sintra; *Price per night*: €203.67
- Sleep In Bucelas—*Location*: Rua Vasco da Gama 32, 2670-633, Bucelas; *Price per night*: €79.64
- Sintra Marmoris Palace—*Location*: Av. Barão de Almeida Santos, 7 Quinta dos Cedros, 2710- 525, Sintra; *Price per night*: €289.85

- Casa Holstein Quinta de São Sebastião Sintra—*Location*: Rua/Travessa São Sebastião, 3, 2710-592, Sintra; *Price per night*: €258.23
- Lisbon Check-In Guesthouse—*Location*: Largo Vitorino Damásio 3-3dto, Estrela; *Price per night*: €124.93
- Lisboa Intendente 3-Bedroom Apartment with Balcony—*Location*: 43 Rua Antero de Quental, Arroios; *Price per night*: €299.89
- C&O Guest House Alcântara-Lisbon—*Location*: Rua José Dias Coelho 20 R/C, esquerdo, Alcântara; *Price per night*: €74.94
- Nova Alegria—*Location*: 5 Rua da Mãe de Água, Santo Antonio; *Price per night*: €137.94
- Beautiful Suite—*Location*: Rua José Falcão Número 34 Segundo Esquerdo, Arroios; *Price per night*: €239.93
- Be Lisbon Residence Marquês—*Location*: Av. António Augusto de Aguiar 56, 1 esq, Avenidas Novas; *Price per night*: €52.95

Best Neighborhoods for Living in Lisbon

When you are thinking about moving to another country, you can start to worry. There are so many unfamiliar aspects to the move, and one of them is not knowing enough about the neighborhood you will be living in. There are so many options when it comes to neighborhoods in Lisbon. You can find a neighborhood close to the city center to experience the buzzing energy of Lisbon central or you can opt for a quieter area with narrow streets in a close-knit local community. There are many neighborhoods in Lisbon, 11 to be exact, and it is up to you to choose which one best suits your needs, budget, and dreams. We have lists of the neighborhoods that are great for the different stages and phases in life while also offering a different lifestyle. If you are wanting to live in an area with many amenities to live a convenient life or maybe keen to go on a little escape outside of the city, we have got you covered!

Family-Friendly Neighborhoods

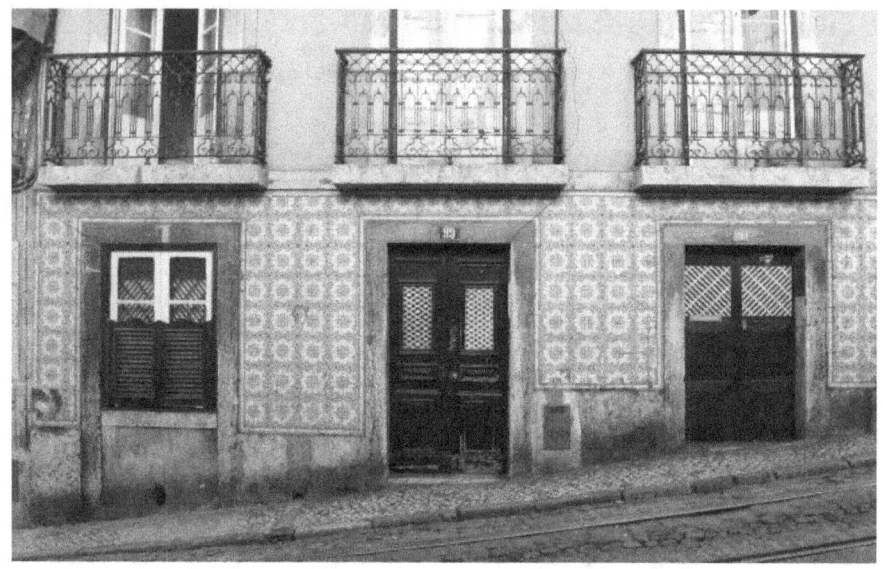

Avenidas Novas

This is a large residential area of Lisbon. The public services and transportation are also very accessible. There are plenty of attractions, amenities, as well as great housing opportunities. The parks and family-friendly layout are what make this neighborhood good for families. The property has seen an increase in price as this neighborhood has grown in development and popularity due to its amenities and universities.

Belém

This neighborhood is very popular as it is a tourist hub to some extent, but it also holds many historical buildings and houses that are owned by locals. There is a sense of community in this neighborhood despite it being a place filled with tourist attractions. It is not the city center and it offers old world charm due to its architecture, making it feel like a place you can call home right away. There are also places for residents to gather, including cafés, restaurants, and bars.

Estrela

This is an older neighborhood and it is much more central. You can feel the rich Portuguese culture in this area with its hills and attractions, including the Jardim Guerra Junqueiro park. You can take Tram 28 to get around this green and charming neighborhood. The local and conveniently located park in the area is a great place for children to spend their hours outside.

Parque das Nações

This neighborhood is quite central and it is easy to commute to the city center via the metro. There are many newer constructions as well as museums and attractions that draw tourists, including the Oceanarium, casino, many restaurants, and bars. The shopping center is also a plus, making this neighborhood even more convenient. The view of the Tagus river from this neighborhood will remind you that you are in Lisbon despite all the newer architecture and new world features. Due to the many amenities and its proximity to the city center, this is a great place to live as a working family.

Alvalade

This neighborhood has a laidback residential feel as it has charming streets offering character-filled buildings and space for greenery. While there are a few cafés and restaurants for locals, this area offers a quieter Lisbon experience even though it is only a 20-minute metro ride away from the city center. The neighborhood feels like you have stepped into a much slower life while still having access to the buzzing city, making it great for families to live in and travel to attractions around the city.

Central and Vibrant City Living

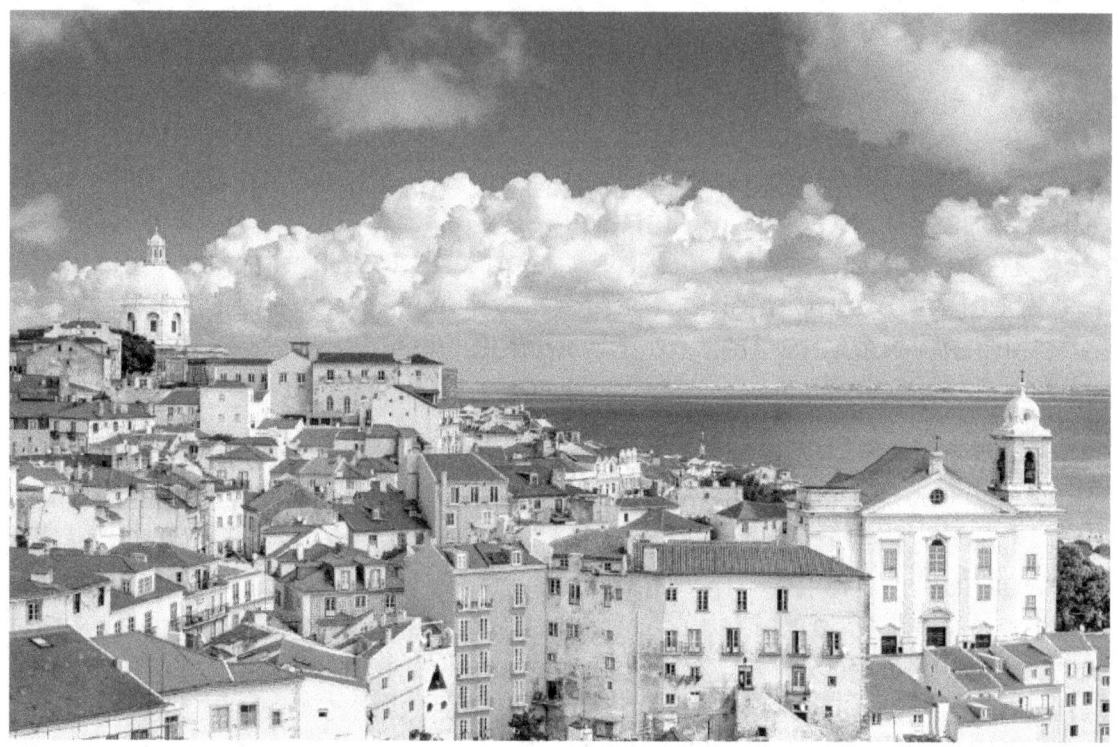

Alfama

This is the oldest district in Lisbon and it carries so much charm and historic elements. The neighborhood and communities here will make you feel like you are living in a Portuguese fairytale. The medieval elements and the narrow cobblestoned streets are a few elements of this area that make it full of traditional Portuguese character. You can feel like you are in a maze that has taken you to another century while you live close to attractions such as the iconic Castelo de São Jorge. The neighborhood is made up of so many different types of people from all walks of life, which is great for an expat to feel part of the city. There are many amenities and trendy cafés and eateries. This neighborhood is a perfect blend of today's vibrant energy and medieval charm. Therefore, the housing reflects this as you may find homes that have been renovated with modern elements as well as some older homes that you can get for a bargain in need of some TLC.

Baixa

This neighborhood is well-positioned as it is part of central Lisbon. This means that you can walk to many attractions and cultural hotspots. There are also local entertainment establishments and attractions, including *ginjinha* bars, the interactive Lisbon Story Center museum, Praça Comércio, and Rua Augusta Arch. The location, bordering the shopping district of Chiado as well as the city center's business hub, and having efficient public transport routes, make this neighborhood a good option if you want to reside in a place that gives you that authentic Lisbon city-living feel.

Bairro Alto

This is a district known for its nightlife and iconic style. The majority of people who spend their time here are locals, singles, party-goers, and young adults. Due to the many bars and eateries, this neighborhood can get quite crowded and noisy. If you are looking for a high-energy place to stay where there is always life and bustling in central Lisbon, this neighborhood is perfect for you. Despite the youthful atmosphere, the architecture and design of the neighborhood are still classic with older buildings and narrow streets. There are many old-world elements to this neighborhood, like the vintage tram that travels to and from the district to Baixa known as the *Elevador da Glória*. The position of this neighborhood offers you some great views of the rest of Lisbon as it is one of the more hilly areas. This neighborhood is filled with local culture and entertainment as you can find a cheap traditional eatery and a bar with live music any day.

Chiado

This area is known for being the shopping hub of Lisbon among tourists and locals. It is connected to the central district of Baixa and offers many amenities, transport routes, and attractions. You can access the Santa Justa Elevator and the iconic Rua da Augusta as well as the Largo do Carmo. Within the neighborhood, you can find an array of cafés and restaurants. There is also the iconic statue of the famous Portuguese poet Fernando Pessoa that draws tourists to take photographs. The neighborhood is unique and offers its own charm, but is in the middle of the hustle and bustle of city life.

Príncipe Real

The name of this neighborhood means Royal Prince and you can see why once you walk down the streets of this very fashionable and sought-after area, which is also connected to the stunning Avenida da Liberdade. There are many local cultural attractions, including some of the city's trendiest restaurants, bars, art galleries, and clothing boutiques. The people who live here are often expats or people who can afford property on the higher end of the price range. The area is in high demand and there is no question as to why it is so sought-after and trendy. The style, layout, amenities, and local attractions are why people want to live here.

Santos

This older neighborhood is also one of the most expensive. The streets are populated with bars and clubs that attract young adults, especially local college students. The neighborhood is an art hub with many design schools and the Ancient Art Museum. The nightlife is vibrant due to the demographic of its residents. During the day, the place sees many tourists because of its architecture, art, churches, and museums.

Rural Areas

Sintra

This is a town outside of Lisbon, but it only takes 30 minutes to get there by train. It is much more quiet than other districts as it is located in a rural mountainous area. In fact, due to its many historical and old buildings, it is a UNESCO World Heritage site and can draw in many tourists who want to take day trips to the town. If you are wanting to live in a smaller town that is not too far from the city, then Sintra is a smart choice. The greenery and old buildings can add to the feeling of tranquility. There are amenities, shops, and restaurants in the area, but it is not as populated or developed compared to the districts of Lisbon. This means that you can get a property here for much less than in the city, although you may need to be ready for a renovation project.

Cascais

This coastal town is out of the city and offers a resort feeling. In fact, it is often called the Portuguese Riviera. The beach attracts many locals and tourists, and of course investors. The marina, nature, and amenities like the train station, make it perfect for expats who have the extra money to spend on property in a more up-market seaside town. The town has preserved its charm while also having newer tourist sights and restaurants. Cascais is a place where tourists come to spend the day from Lisbon to enjoy its beaches and laid back vibe. It is a much more exclusive area and property prices here are expensive, but you do get more for your money compared to living in the city center. It is also possible to live here and work in Lisbon as the commute is not that long. Therefore, you can enjoy both the advantages of the city as well as the calming effect of coastal living.

Chapter 6: Travel and Transport

Getting Around the City

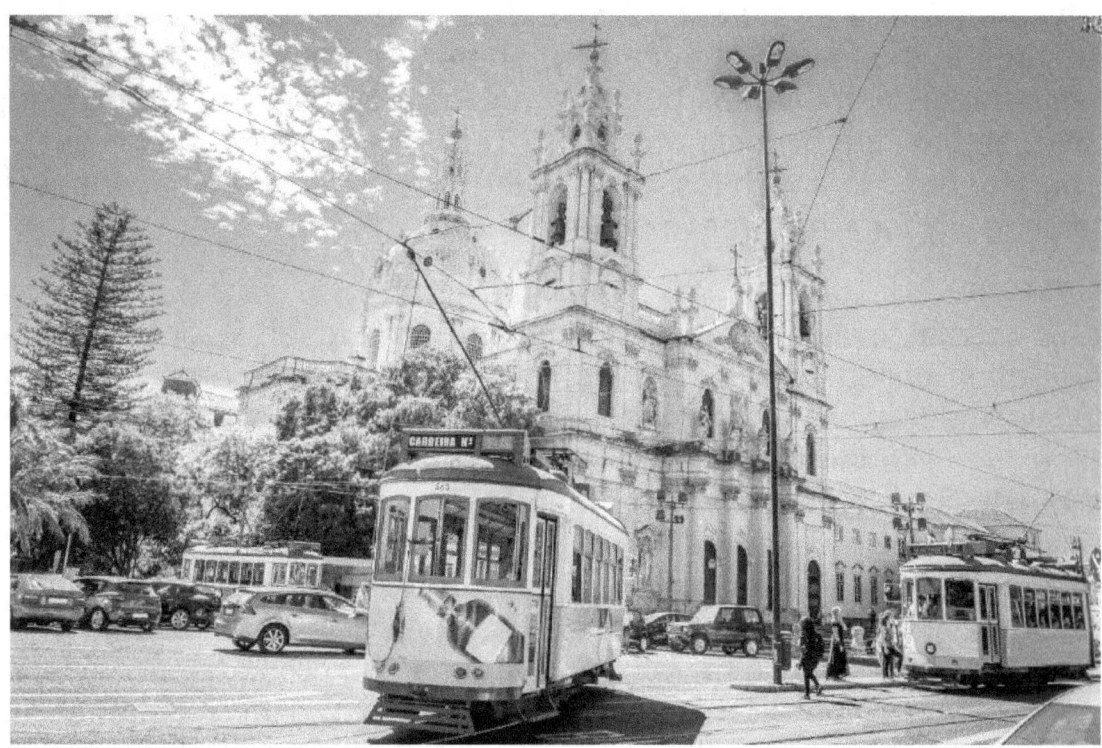

Modes of Transport

Lisbon, like any big city, offers an array of efficient and popular public transport options. The most used modes of transport include trams, the metro, buses, and trains, with the most popular being moving around the city by foot. The transport in Lisbon is accessible and affordable as you can purchase a travel card to use for the length of your stay with no limitations. You can purchase a reusable card, known as a "Viva Viagem" card to get around using all modes of public transport, such as the metro, trams, and buses for 24 hours, which is perfect for sightseeing. A Lisboa Card is also a good option that provides unlimited rides of public transport lasting for 24, 48, and even 72 hours. This card also gives you access to some discounts on attractions, tours, and museum entrance fees.

Let us look at and then compare some of the popular modes of public transport available in Lisbon:

- Trams: This a convenient way to get around the central areas of the city. You can be in the middle of the city and get to specific streets. You will be immersed in the culture as you travel the tram with different types of people between the many old roads of the city. The price for a single fare can work out to be €3 if you buy it on board from the driver, but it works out cheaper if you use a travel card. The trams travel through popular areas of the city and must-see districts you need to visit when on vacation, including Baixa, Alfama, Estrela, and Graça.
- The metro: This the fastest way to get around the city. There are 55 stations and four lines that operate around Lisbon from 6:60 am to 1:00 am.
- Buses: This is another inexpensive mode of transport. Like the tram, a single fare costs €1.50. There are 172 bus routes and these run from 5:00 am to 1:00 am. You can also top up your "Viva Viagem" before you travel around for the day. To make sure the bus stops for you, you can wave your hands so that the driver does not drive past you. The bus is a cost-effective option when it comes to traveling in Lisbon, but is not as efficient or fast as the metro and trams.

- Trains: This is a good option when traveling long distances or when you want to do day trips. You can travel to and from different municipalities by train. The train stations that are popular when traveling to different municipalities and even cities include stations Oriente and Cais do Sodré. These day trips usually cost around €2 or even less. The train lines also run through Lisbon central, Sintra, Azambuja, and Sado.

While local taxis and transport services are available, these tend to be more costly. Many taxis are known to be tourist traps as they overcharge many foreigners. While making use of an app and ordering a lift on your mobile device is a little cheaper than getting a local taxi, it requires an internet connection and the cost works out to be more in the long-term compared to using public transportation.

Lisbon Travel Tips

- Use public transport to save money.
- Accept that you will need to walk to and from most places.
- Buying a bus and/or tram ticket from the drive is more expensive than buying a ticket at the station via a ticket machine or a cashier.
- The smart choice to get around the city is by using a Viva Viagem Card which you can purchase at a metro or train station.
- Making use of funiculars and lifts in the hilly city of Lisbon is a great way to view attractions.
- Ferries are operational, efficient, and affordable when traveling to islands for sightseeing adventures.
- Choose a taxi if it is your last and only option as they can be much more expensive than other transport options.

- Booking a rental car in advance so that you can do day trips outside of the city will save you money while also making your adventures more convenient.
- Carry some cash on you to cover any unforeseen tickets, entrance fees, or additional travel costs.

Popular and Scenic Travel Routes

If you have a rental car and want to take a drive around the Lisbon region or go on a day trip out of the the busy city, then you may appreciate the list below that consists of some of our top favorite routes that travelers can take to experience the breathtaking views and a little refreshing change of scenery:

1. The N379, through Serra da Arrabida
2. The N247, between Azóia and Cascais
3. The N6 to Cascais
4. The Ponte 25 de Abril Bridge

If you are wanting to do a road trip and then reach a spectacular destination, below is a list of some of our the best road trip drives and destinations you can take from Lisbon:

- Cascais: To reach this old town with its blue waters and stunning cliffs, you can drive down the N6 west from Lisbon. On your way, you will also pass other small beach towns, including Paco de Arcos and Estoril. Your destination, as well as your journey, will be a treat as you drive past the unspoiled natural treasures of Portugal's coastal region. This is a popular day trip and it deserves to be! Once you reach Cascais, you can lounge on one of its beaches or walk through the old town

center. There is so much to do as it is so worth the drive out of the city.
- Peniche: This small city is located along the coast, in the Oeste region. It is a popular surfing spot, but there are also other attractions that you can admire, including the nature reserve and all its natural beauties as well as the historic buildings of the city center. You can also take a boat ride to reach Berlenga Grande island, which also has its own history as a former prison. The trip from Lisbon takes just over an hour via the A8.
- Quinta da Regaleira: Located near the old town of Sintra, you can explore this UNESCO heritage site. While your drive can include Sintra, you can also add this Gothic palace to your list of must-see attractions. There are many photographs that have been taken of this unique 19th century palace as it is covered with different plants and as many secret tunnels, making it a spiraling labyrinth that transports you to a different place.
- Tomar: You can take the A1 to get to Tomar in about an hour and 30 minutes, and then spend the rest of the day exploring the historic buildings of the riverside town. The town's most popular attraction is the Convento de Cristo, which is a 12th century fortified convent. The town is charming with cobbled streets and unique architecture.
- Serra da Arrabida: If you take the scenic route, driving down the N379, you can pass the many hills of the Lisbon region until you reach this natural park in 50 minutes. This is a trip you can do when the weather is pleasant so that you can walk around the park and spend hours roaming its 10, 500 hectares. There are hills that meet the beach, another place you can spend hours at. The best beaches in this specific region are definitely Figueirinha, Galapinhos, and Creiro. If you are

wanting to take a scenic drive out of the city to experience a relaxing day out in nature, then this route is for you.
- **Ponte 25 de Abril bridge and surrounding areas:** This route is a unique experience and stands out among the rest due to the views it offers you. You can cross the bridge, just about a mile out of the city, and experience the breathtaking views of Lisbon. To get to the viewpoint, you will need to drive down the A2 to leave the city center until you reach the bridge in just 15 minutes. Due to the location of the bridge, it is a popular tourist site that offers great photography opportunities. If you want to take a short drive out of the city to get a different view, then this is a smart route to follow.

Traveling From Lisbon to Lagos

While Lisbon is one of the best cities to travel to and around, there are other regions of Portugal that offer unique experiences and their own local attractions that are so different to those you will find in Lisbon. Traveling from Lisbon to other cities or smaller towns is more popular than you might think. Day trips out of the city to nature reserves and old towns are common, and so is traveling from the city to Lagos, about 115 miles south of Lisbon. There are actually three transportation options available when traveling from Lisbon to Lagos, which are the bus, the train, or by car.

If you are vacationing in Portugal and do not have a rental car, there is inexpensive public transport available for this specific route. You can either take the bus or the train from Lisbon to Lagos. The bus provides a direct route from Lisbon to Lagos, while the train has a connecting trip that is located in the small town of Tunes. Whichever option you choose would depend on your travel preferences, including comfort, timing, and scheduling.

Things to Know About Inter-Regional Travel

Due to Covid-19, the last two years have changed the way we travel internationally as well as domestically. There have been protocols or limitations concerning inter-regional travel throughout Portugal. As restrictions have begun to ease, the travel restrictions have been lifted. Currently, people can move freely in and around Portugal. Of course, certain protocols may need to be followed, including the wearing of face masks in closed public places or the expectation to sanitize surfaces or your hands in certain circumstances. There are many ways to get around the country and travel from one district to the other, or one city to the next.

There are different bus companies that offer rides to Lagos, and the average travel time is under four hours, yet this may vary depending on which route the specific bus follows. The prices of bus tickets are relatively cheap, with a single fare costing around €20 on average. There are some well-serviced buses that offer comfortable and modern journeys. You should book your bus ticket in advance so that you can select your seats, and sometimes you can get some good online discounts. There are different private bus tour companies, but the main intercity bus company that offers rides across the country is Rede Expresso which has acquired other bus companies in recent years. Rede Expresso has many routes and stations, being the most reliable and accessible company. You can go online and look at their seasonal timetables and book tickets before your cross-country or local journey.

The train offers a more spacious journey. It also has its own line which makes for a scenic trip across the country. Train fares are usually similar to bus fares, but depending on the length of the journey and the type of carriage you pick, you can spend more or less than you would on a bus ticket. For instance, first class tickets cost around €30 while second class tickets a few euros less at €23 for a single adult fare. Like the bus, you would need to pre-book your tickets before the day of your departure in order to select your seats.

Chapter 7: Discover Lisbon's Natural Beauty

Lisbon's Beaches

Must-See, Popular, and Isolated Beaches

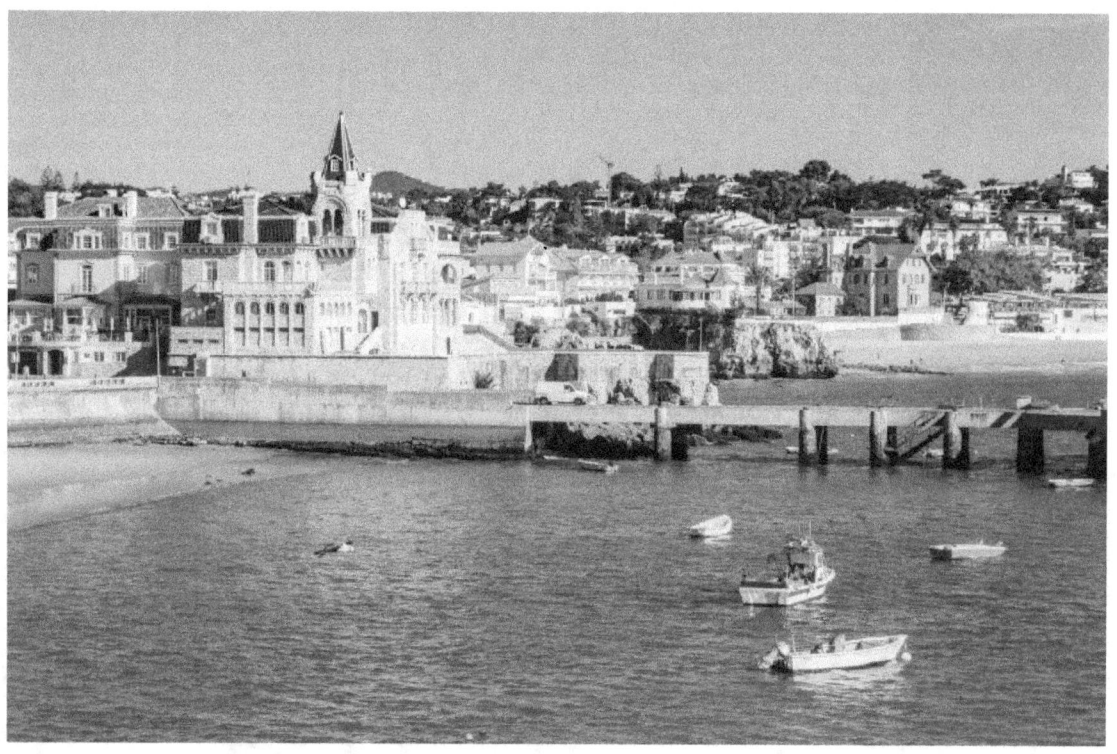

- *Praia de Carcavelos*: This is a beach, 35 minutes from Lisbon center, and it is on the Atlantic. It's the biggest and most popular, especially among young tourists, as the beach is perfect for surfing and other beach sports, including beach volleyball. The beach is quite popular, and tourists and locals alike gather here when the weather is pleasant, so it can get crowded on weekends and throughout the summer.

- *Praia do Creiro*: This is one of the popular beaches in the region despite being an hour outside of the city center. With calm and clear waters, people can swim and sunbathe for hours. It also neighbors other lovely beaches, so the location is great if you are in the mood for some beach hopping.
- *Praia da Conceição*: This beach in Cascais is loved by tourists as it is close to the train station and has a promenade that is connected to other beaches. The waters are calm which makes it perfect for swimming and lounging all day. Due to its location, this beach can often get crowded, so it is perfect for convenience, but not your go-to beach for a quiet beach escape.
- *Praia do Tamariz*: Just over 30 minutes outside of the city center, you will find this popular beach across from a castle and a grand casino. There are many facilities surrounding the beach, including hotels, beach bars, restaurants, and even a train station. Due to its location, this beach has remained one of the more popular beaches situated around the city of Lisbon.
- *Praia da Adraga*: This stunning beach is more secluded and surrounded by rocks instead of beach bars and tourist hubs. It has been said to be one of the most beautiful beaches in Europe as it still remains wild and untouched, so the natural beauty of Lisbon's seaside is really showcased. Locals choose to spend their days here as it is quieter, away from tourists and almost empty on weekdays, yet it can get busier on weekends.

- *Praia da Figuerinha*: Located outside of Lisbon in Setúbal, this beach is perfect for a family trip or a group outing. This beach stands out as it is located along green hills and it also has a lagoon, which makes it a sheltered beach, perfect for children. The ocean water is calm and so clear that you can spot fish right at your feet.
- *Praia da Rainha*: This beach is one of the stunning beaches in Cascais. While it is close to the city, about 45 minutes from the center of Lisbon, you can escape to crystal clear waters and bronze sand sheltered by rocks. The beach is perfect for sunbathing and soaking up the atmosphere of Cascais. It is close to the train station and faces the harbor. It offers opportunities for relaxation or getting some good Instagram-worthy snaps.
- *Costa da Caparica*: This beach, with its long stretch of soft sand and pleasant water, is close to the city center and is very popular. It is often crowded and it has been divided into sections, with one dedicated to nudists. There are many beach bars along this stretch that makes for a great nightlife with many trendy establishments offering drinks and music. If you are looking for a relaxing day out by the sea that turns into a fun night out after sunset, this beach will give you all that and more.
- *Praia dos Galapinhos*: This beach is a sweet escape from the city and is close to many other popular beaches. Its waters and surrounding landscape make it look like a postcard. While it is close to other beaches, it is never as crowded, so you can enjoy the calm water as well as a quiet area to lie and relax under the sun.
- *Praia do Guincho*: Part of the Sintra-Cascais Natural Park, this windy beach is a popular spot for water sports, including

windsurfing. The beach is not as crowded as others that are close to it, but it is loved by surfers. If you are interested in surfing or just want to enjoy a meal at one of the popular seafood restaurants in the area, you can take a 1-hour trip out of Lisbon to visit this beach with stunning views and sand dunes.

- *Meco*: This is one of the most popular nude beaches in Portugal. The beach is surrounded by a pine forest and cliffs. The water can get rough, so it is not ideal for swimming. The soft sand and its dunes make it a perfect place to sunbathe.
- *Praia do Ribeiro do Cavalo*: To reach this beach it takes about under an hour by car with an extra 20-minute hike to get to the shore. The walk is worth it as the beach offers great views, a doable trail, and calm waters as a treat after your walk. It would be a good idea to spend an afternoon or hours here as it is not easy to get to. You can go in a group and make a day out of it with a picnic. The water is calm and a stunning blue, making it a stunning view to admire in itself.
- *Praia da Ursa*: You can find this isolated beach between Sintra and Cascais. To reach the secluded beach of sea stacks, you need to follow a trail down a cliff and down to the shore. The beach is a perfect picnic spot or a local treasure to explore, but not for swimming as the waves are strong and the rocks and shoreline do not make it safe to swim. The beach is unique and worth it if you are looking for a quick coastal adventure during a day trip outside of the city.

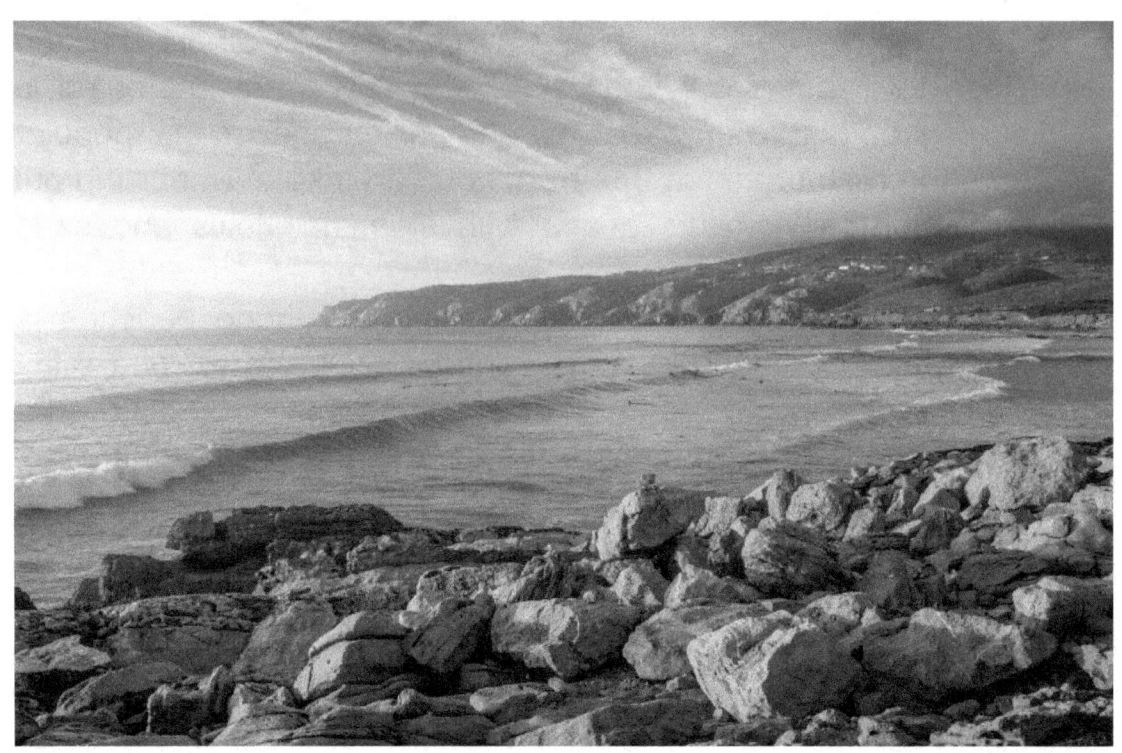

Tours and Trails

Nature Reserves and Hiking Trails

Reserves and Parks

- *Sintra-Cascais Natural Park*: This is a must-see when taking a day trip out of Lisbon. The Parque Natural de Sintra Cascais is a natural beauty, almost like Portugal's all-natural art museum that is about 17,000 hectares. The park consists of dunes in Guincho as well as the stunning hills of Sintra. The landscape showcases the diversity of fauna and flora of this region of Portugal as there are sand dunes as well as a lush valley of pine trees. The hills of this park border the Atlantic ocean, and there are forests and sea caves all in one area. You can experience the ocean sound as well as the luscious woods of the valley and forest as if you can travel through two worlds in one day, which is possible when in the Sintra-Cascais region.

- *Tagus Estuary Natural Reserve:* The Reserva Natural do Estuário do Tejo, is on the south bank of the Tagus river just outside the city of Lisbon. Here, you will discover the largest wetland in Portugal which is home to thousands of birds as the area is made up of mud, marshes, and salt pans. The banks attract migrating flamingos in fall, while you can spot so many different types of birds throughout the year. This is a lovely and convenient escape into nature while being on the doorstep of the city, making it a perfect getaway when you are in the mood for some fresh air and exploration outside of the busy city.

- *EVOA-Tagus Estuary Birdwatching and Conservation Area*: If you are an avid birdwatcher, or if you are just interested in the indigenous birds of the Tagus region, then visiting this estuary should be on your travel list. You can spend time observing the birds in their natural habitat, a protected wetland in Tagus. This is a much-needed escape, a day trip that invites you to slow down and focus on nature instead of the over-stimulating distractions of the city. The estuary is just 30 minutes outside of Lisbon. A guided tour costs anywhere between €5 to €12 per person, which is a smart option as you can learn more about the wildlife, history, and significance of the wetland. There is also an exhibition area with information about the estuary as well as a cafeteria for your convenience.

- *Sado Estuary Nature Reserve*: Known as the Reserva Natural do Estuário do Sado, this nature reserve is outside of Lisbon and is a magnificent place to visit as you take a road trip out of

the city to Arrábida or Setúbal. The landscape, with a perfect balance of hilltops and shoreline, not only provides amazing views, but it also brings with it many different animals. The coastal wetland that makes this area unique is also home to many sea animals, including seabirds and dolphins. You can spend time birding or walking past the surprising rice paddies and greener woods that you will never be able to experience in the city. Due to its more isolated location, along the Tróia peninsula, there is an abundance of indigenous and even threatened wildlife, including local sea otters and the black bat in this conservation area. There is a ferry that can take you across the peninsula to catch sight of this amazing area, or you can spend the day in the estuary so that you can dedicate enough time to be immersed in the wildlife of this reserve.
- *Arrábida Natural Park*: Just outside of Setúbal you can spend a day in this peaceful park. The park is situated where the land and sea meet, attracting many local animals and tourists looking for a more tranquil experience in Portugal's most calming reserve. If you are looking to explore the natural beauty outside of the fishing town of Setúbal, you can explore the reserve which has walking trails and offers you a unique display of birds, butterflies, and other indigenous animals. Here, you can spend the day among the fauna and flora among the hills as well as the calming and more isolated beaches.

Hiking Trails

- *Sintra to Colares*: This trail is part of the Sintra mountain range, near the old town of Sintra, just outside the city of Lisbon. The trail is just under 7 miles in distance and is in the form of a loop. If you have gone hiking before, this trail would be a good option. It might not be the best for beginners or for families with small children as it is considered more of a moderate trail than easy. The distance and time it takes, over three hours, makes it a popular trail among hikers and those who are adventure lovers throughout the year. Despite the many benefits of walking in nature, this route also has its own advantages, including the views of the Sintra Palace, Castelo dos Mouros, and the Pena National Palace.

- *Barragem do Rio da Mula*: This is a pedestrian route found in the Sintra-Cascais Natural Park. This walk is moderately challenging and is also perfect for walking, running, or cycling. The distance is 5 miles in distance, which would take you about two hours and 30 minutes. You can also enjoy the park and its diverse flora. The park is a protected area, so this trail is perfect for a pair or small groups.
- *Albufeira do Rio da Mula*: The trail is near the Sintra region, with views overlooking the mountain range. This is an easy, family-friendly trail which also welcomes dogs. The distance of this loop is 6 miles and takes under three hours to complete. This is a great outing for the family or for groups as it also caters for mountain biking. Along the route, you can admire the Mula River reservoir as well as wild or farm animals, including horses, cows, and donkeys.
- *Rota do Litoral do Guincho*: In the Parque Natural de Sintra-Cascais, you can walk this route where the hills and beach meet within the Sintra mountain range. This is a moderate trail and about 6 miles in distance, taking an average of two hours and 30 minutes. You can enjoy the natural beauty surrounding Sintra or explore the village of Malveira da Serra. The historical buildings and pure, natural landscapes in the reserve.
- *Rota Circular da Pedra Amarela*: This is an easy trail in the Pedra Amarela area. It is a forestry walk and perfect for

families with children or anyone who wants to partake in a stroll through the woods in Sintra. The distance is under 4 miles, which will only take under two hours to walk. You can take your time to soak up the goodness of the forest of the Sintra region with all its tranquility, wildlife, and simplicity contrasting the city of Lisbon.

Unique Experiences

Once in a Lifetime Adventures

Portuguese Pilgrims Walk to Santiago de Compostela

The Portuguese Camino de Santiago is a well-known spiritual journey across Portugal. People from all over the world travel to do this pilgrimage, known as The Way of Saint James, to follow the route of the pilgrims to the shrine of the apostle St. James the Great. This trail takes weeks to complete, but there are different routes you can take to reach your destination, the cathedral of Santiago de Compostela, so the distance will vary depending on which option you choose. The central route is about 160 miles, making it the shortest journey. The second option is to walk along the coast, with a distance of 174 miles. The longest route starts from Lisbon, which requires you to walk a distance of about 390 miles, making the journey take almost double the time. In general, the pilgrimage can take up to two weeks, while the route from Lisbon to the cathedral takes over 20 days. There are many places to stop and explore along the way. It is advised to travel in a group and be well-prepared as the difficulty level for this journey is challenging and not on the same level as a moderate day hike. The Camino is definitely a journey that you will never forget!

Snorkeling in Arrábida Natural Park

If you love being in the water or have an interest in marine life, then going on a day trip to snorkel in Arrábida is a unique adventure perfect for you. You can book a snorkeling session and dive in the clear waters of the Atlantic Ocean to observe the wildlife of Arrábida that exists under the sea. The park is a wildlife conservation area that also includes a mountain range and coastline that you can also explore as you follow the trails leading you through the hills and valleys of this special coastal region.

Walk to and around Fátima

The old city of Fátima is central to one of the popular multiple-day routes in and around Lisbon. Known as the "city of peace," Fátima is a pilgrimage destination as well as a historic place of interest travelers can explore on a day trip as it is a sanctuary commemorating the Virgin of Fátima. There are different routes one can take to reach the city, with the shortest route known as the Nazaré route, dedicated to Our Lady Nazaré, being 2 days long. The route that starts in Lisbon takes 5 days to complete, but along the way you can travel through stunning mountain ranges and the unspoiled valleys that are located between the Tagus River and the Atlantic Ocean.

Visit the Schist Villages

Located between Lisbon and Porto, you can take a day trip through Coimbra to discover the unique houses made of *schist*, a specific metamorphic rock, in the mountainous area of Serra de Lousã. The villages, also found in Açor, Zêzere, and Tejo-Ocreza will make you feel that you have been transported into another time, another world. The buildings are so old yet keep their structure, maybe this is why these villages are referred to as the places where the "secrets of Portugal are kept." These structures, built between the 12th and 13th centuries, have stood the test of time, and we can only imagine what those schist walls have seen throughout the centuries. The houses make up small shepherds' cottages and there are also narrow alleys that connect the houses. This day trip offers a rare experience, a historical display like no other.

Chapter 8: Traveling During Covid-19

The world has changed so much over the past two years, and so has the way we connect with others, work, and go about our recreational activities. In the last two years, we have had to adjust how we do our daily tasks to prevent the spread of a contagious virus, which has automatically led us to avoid social gatherings. The pandemic has restricted our movement and we have seen how many countries created local and international travel policies specifically focused on curbing the spread of Covid-19. You may ask yourself how your trip to Lisbon will be like in 2022... Well, things have started to look brighter and places have opened up to the local public as well as international travelers. Lisbon is open for you to come and enjoy all it has to offer, as long as you remember to adapt to its local protocols and remain cautious and respect the social etiquette and laws of the city.

Covid-19 Travel Tips

Traveling during a pandemic adds an additional factor to your preparation for your trip. While we have all needed to adapt our daily lives since the beginning of the pandemic, travel and movement have also been affected. Therefore, your daily behavior, specifically in public places, when on holiday or anywhere for that matter, has needed to change to prevent the spread of Covid-19. Below is a list of general precautions you can take to make your trip during a pandemic a little less stressful and overwhelming:

- Check the Covid-19 policies of your destination.
- Research the travel requirements for international and regional flying, specifically vaccination cards or Covid tests, before

leaving for your trip.
- Look out for signs about sanitizing, distancing, and wearing masks in public places and establishments like restaurants or hotels.
- Be sure to carry a mask, negative covid results, or proof of vaccination when you are traveling in case you get stopped by security.
- Follow basic hygiene, including washing hands or sanitizing regularly.
- Look for sanitized and cleaned accommodation with preventative measures.
- To protect yourself, maintain a healthy immune system by following a nutritious diet or taking a multivitamin.
- Trust your gut when it comes to eating out at new eateries; if you feel that the utensils are not clean enough, then ask for a new set or avoid eating at places you think may not follow basic hygiene principles in their kitchens.

Updated Portuguese Travel Policies and Protocol

Every country has its own policies created to combat the spread of the Covid-19 virus. The entire world has been affected by the contagious virus, but each country and its regions and cities have followed different approaches according to their own current situation. Depending on the population size of a place and the culture of the people, local policies and protocol may differ from place to place. Lisbon falls under Portuguese law and has implemented the country's Covid-19 policies. Therefore, when you travel around Lisbon you need to follow the rules that the country and city have in place to prevent the spread of Covid-19 to ensure locals' and tourists' safety and health are a priority.

Portugal is open for non-essential travel, which is tourist travel, while essential travel includes a valid reason for your stay, including work, a specific program, studies, or immigration. If you are traveling from a country of the European Union, presenting an EU Digital COVID Certificate is enough to enter the country. If you are not traveling from these countries, before you can enter Portugal, you will need to present a proof of an approved vaccination with either a QR code on your mobile phone and/or a vaccine card. The vaccinations accepted by EU countries include vaccines produced by BioNTech and Pfizer, Novavax, Moderna, AstraZeneca, Vero Cell, Coronavac, and Covaxin. If you do not have a vaccination card for these vaccines, you will need to present a negative rapid test that was taken in the 24 hours prior to your boarding time *or* a negative NAAT test that was performed within 72 hours before boarding time. You will not be permitted to enter the country without one of these valid documents, and will be fined as well as sent on a return journey on the next available. If you test positive for Covid-19, you will need to quarantine in a hotel for 10 days before you can travel around the country.

Currently, people are free to move around cities and travel across national borders to different regions of the country. There is no curfew and bars as well as clubs are currently in operation. Public indoor facilities that hold groups of people are allowed to hold their full capacity. Therefore shopping malls and restaurants are open to the public and have no restrictions on the number of people who are allowed to enter. Cafés, bars, restaurants, theaters, and other social events can operate at normal trading hours at their full capacity of their specific venues. Gatherings like weddings and other celebrations are also permitted without restrictions concerning the number of people present.

While movement, social gathering, and mask wearing are not controlled like before, it is still mandatory to wear masks in certain places like health facilities and public transportation. People are also encouraged to be cautious and practice safe social distancing and socializing in general. Fines can be issued when one is not complying with the local Covid protocols or when one fails to present a Covid-19 test on their arrival at a Portuguese airport. The Covid-19 policies of Portugal have been implemented to protect their citizens, maintain a functioning society and economy, as well as prevent tourists from falling ill. With over 90% of the population vaccinated, the country has been able to control the spread of the virus as well as successfully combat it and protect people who are in Portugal. By following the protocol encouraged by the Portuguese government and by being wise about your behavior, your stay in the country can be an enjoyable and safe experience.

Chapter 9: Local Lisbon Living

Learn About the People and Places

The people of Lisbon are definitely not homogenous, as there are people from all over the world, with different cultures and languages, who come together and live to the fullest in this city. While Lisbon is a cosmopolitan city, it is still the heart of Portugal. The city still preserves its own history and unique Portuguese culture. With the Portuguese language, there is a way to connect and communicate with people in a specific way that carries the culture with it.

One way to learn more about the local people of the city is to learn the language they speak. You can know so much about people when you learn their language and begin to understand them a bit better. Speaking English to locals and tourists or expats is the best way to meet new people and learn more about others and the city. Therefore, learning some useful Portuguese phrases, and spending time with locals and expats who have lived in the city for a while would help you get to know the people around you and the place you are living in.

Another reason to make use of Portuguese and English is the fact that speaking these languages will help you get to know the places and streets of the city. Asking for directions in Portuguese or English will be the most efficient way to get orientated when exploring the city. Another way to learn more about the places you find yourself in is to do some research before you start your expedition. You should also make use of map apps to help you with navigation and finding your way around the different streets. Make sure that you stay up to date with the places and their locations or addresses by looking up the places you will visit or finding out from locals as some establishments move their locations or even close down. This is a very important factor when getting acclimated, especially due to the economic toll of the Covid-19 pandemic. Many businesses have had to close down, move, downscale, or change the way they operate. Therefore, make sure you talk to locals and look up opening times and recent reviews of places on your web browser or stay updated via social media.

Below are some tips and tricks to learning more about the layout, places, and people of Lisbon:

- Download map apps.
- Talk to locals and expats.
- Make use of social media to learn about what people are saying and doing in the city's establishments.
- Skim through local news articles via a news app.

- Observe people by sitting in a busy place and allowing yourself to be immersed in the city and its energy.
- Do not be afraid to approach the person behind the help desk.
- Talk to the host, receptionist, or security of your accommodation.
- Book a guided tour of the city.
- Eat out where the locals go and hang out where the locals hang out.
- Wander the streets and do a self-guided walk to fully experience the buzzing city, even if you do get lost.
- Go to popular *fado* houses.
- Use public transport to get used to the different stops, stations, and routes around the city.

This list includes a few ways you can learn about the people and culture of Lisbon, while also becoming more accustomed to the unique lifestyle and social norms that are totally different to your hometown. The cultural shocks or surprises you may experience are all part of the joys of traveling internationally, so remain open-minded and excited about your Lisbon experiences instead of worrying about your mistakes or overthinking while you are on a glorious tour around this amazing city. With time you will find your way and Lisbon will feel like your second home.

Dos and Don'ts of Lisbon Travel

Dos	Don'ts
• Walk around or take public transport. • Drink tap water or filtered water from a reusable water bottle. • Go to popular Fado houses.	• Expect to drive or be driven everywhere. • Boast, brag, or show superiority.

• Learn a few Portuguese phrases or take language classes. • Remain polite when interacting with locals. • Respect or take part in Christian and Catholic traditions. • Dress modestly and with classic clothes, and dress appropriately for the time and place i.e. wear a swimsuit and flip flops at the beach, wear closed shoes when at a restaurant. • Tip waiters with some extra cash and leave it on the table after eating out. • Shake hands and make eye contact when meeting and greeting new people. • Try new foods and remain open-minded.	• Speak Spanish or assume people speak English. • Wear revealing clothes in public. • Say please and thank you too much when ordering at an eatery. • Bring up politics, specifically national politics, in a conversation without the other person bringing it up first. • Assume that you can sunbathe topless on public beaches. • Make cultural comparisons in front of Portuguese people about their own culture and another.

Local Customs

When you are interacting with local people or if you really want to become part of the everyday life of a Portuguese city like Lisbon, you will need to follow the local customs. While people are usually friendly and hospitable to visitors, it is best to observe how people live and learn how to do it the Portuguese way. When in Portugal, do it the Portuguese way! There are a few customs, etiquette, and traditions that are followed in Lisbon. Learning these will help both you and the Portuguese locals around you when you are living in the city.

First of all, learning the greetings and etiquette around strangers or acquaintances will be the most helpful as you will interact with people on a daily basis. When you greet people, it is best to use a popular Portuguese greeting. If you do not know a word of Portuguese, your second option would be English as most people in big cities are used to the language and know the basics. When meeting people for the first time, it is good to give them a strong handshake and keep eye contact as you greet them. If you are greeting friends, a simple pat on the back between men or a kiss on the right and then left cheek between women are acceptable. In formal settings, handshakes are performed at the beginning and end of a meeting.

Communication is important when trying to meet new people and make local connections. Body language and using one's hands a lot when talking are not common. Instead, people speak politely and passionately. Direct communication and being polite are both very much appreciated by locals. While speaking with your hands is not necessary, your position when speaking to someone matters. Personal space needs to be respected in formal settings, while many people are physically closer and touch each other when talking to friends and family. It is normal to see public displays of affection between people, especially couples or friends.

Dining etiquette is always important when dining out at local establishments, no matter where you travel to. Food and manners go hand-in-hand in all sorts of cultures and places. Therefore, when you are in Lisbon, you need to follow the unwritten dining rules of the culture. If you are invited to dinner or out to a gathering, arriving on time is not necessary. It is acceptable to arrive within 15 minutes after the set time. When you are invited to parties or larger gatherings, there is nothing wrong with arriving 30 minutes to even an hour later than the set time. When eating or socializing with others, it is good to follow their lead and remember to not bring up serious topics like politics or business when you are connecting with people in a more relaxed setting. Giving a gift like flowers or chocolate to your host is a decent and appreciated gesture if you are having a cooked meal at someone's house. Remember that table manners are important when eating at a dinner table. Following people's lead and not being obnoxious and forward is seen as polite in most social settings, especially when eating at a table for a meal with Portuguese people. Standing before you are invited to sit down is also common, as well as eating after you are gestured to eat with a host saying *bom apetite* or when others begin to tuck into their meals.

Conclusion

This guide aimed to give you insight into exploring, vacationing, and even settling down in the Portuguese city of Lisbon. Planning for a trip to another country can be overwhelming but also exciting, so it is best to be prepared and informed while also being open to the endless possibilities that you may experience when traveling. The goal here is to avoid as many complications and discover the positive aspects of traveling, and that is why we have given you all you need to know before you leave for Lisbon. Of course there will always be the unforeseen as well as the spontaneous experiences, but with enough preparation and an open mind, your trip to Lisbon can be the most amazing traveling experience.

The city is welcoming and offers so much to so many different types of travelers. In Chapter 1, we discussed how special this city truly is while briefly going through the background of Lisbon. Learning a little bit of history about a place you plan to travel to will only make your trip richer and more enjoyable. In this chapter, we also focused on the ways you can travel around the city, which include some travel tips to help you navigate the life of a traveler in Lisbon. Whether you are a first-time traveler or a self-proclaimed international nomad, there is always a learning opportunity that you can take.

Every city has its own energy, culture, unwritten rules, and tourist traps. This is why we also went through some tourist traps you should be aware of so that you can avoid any uncomfortable situations or setbacks. Preparing and being aware are so important when planning a trip and even when you have already arrived at your destination. Therefore, we gave you some tips and a template to follow when creating your own itinerary, so that you can plan and live out the holiday of your dreams.

In Chapter 2, we looked at some annual events, festivals, and activities you can partake in for each month and season of the year. Lisbon is a tourist hub, so it caters for tourists as well as locals and expats, ensuring that everyone living in the city can enjoy themselves and experience special moments. Depending on your travel wishlist, budget, and preferences, you can find an activity that will make your trip enjoyable, immersive, and so much more memorable. Lisbon is a charming and eclectic city, and there is always something going on. From traditional fado music shows to electronic festivals for the music lovers, to stunning beaches and hiking trails for the nature lovers. The city and its surrounding areas are so diverse. It is possible to get the best of both worlds on your Lisbon trip.

From our overview of the many events that Lisbon has to offer, we listed some of the many must-see attractions and gems that just need to be admired and explored. In Chapter 3, we went through some of the popular attractions that are on display all over the city. From must-see attractions to the many hidden but special streets of Lisbon, this chapter covered the places of interest for any traveler. If you are interested in history and architecture, the many cathedrals and palaces found around Lisbon will draw you in, and you will find yourself wandering through the many passages and chapels for hours. The historic towns just outside of the city with their alleys and charming buildings are also perfect for a day trip dedicated to learning about the stories, events, and background of Portugal's people and communities. If fun nights out in high-energy places are for you, we listed some popular streets that are lined with bars, restaurants, and traditional fado houses.

Chapter 4 was dedicated to the foodies and those who are interested in tasting the unique flavors of traditional Portuguese cuisine. In this chapter, we compiled a few lists of the top restaurants in Lisbon. If you are in the mood to dine out, there are many eateries to choose from. You can spend an evening of fine dining at a Michelin star restaurant, or you can enjoy a hearty meal at a small local kitchen where the owners greet you and serve you as their guests. The food culture in Portugal is diverse and you can find decent and inexpensive meals at markets, delis, or budget-friendly restaurants.

We also looked at ways you can eat and shop like a local, which not only saves you money, but also allows you to feel part of the authentic Portuguese way of enjoying a meal. The food of a city comes with its culture, and that is why we also added some unique and authentically Portuguese culinary experiences you can try out. From cooking with a local chef, to exploring the neighborhood markets or wineries, this chapter has you covered whenever you are feeling like treating your tastebuds or just famished and in need of a wholesome *prego*.

In Chapter 5, we focused on accommodations and the many neighborhoods you can choose from when planning a holiday or moving to Lisbon. Depending on your itinerary, interests, and budget, we provided a variety of holiday accommodations that are currently available to book or rent. When booking an accommodation, you need to think about its amenities and proximity to where you would like to be or where you see yourself exploring. There are different types of accommodations that we went through, including hotels, hostels, and homestays. Depending on your needs and comfort levels, there are so many options out there, but here we only gave you a taster of the many amazing accommodations you can find in Lisbon.

If you are looking to settle in Lisbon and make it your permanent residence, there are many amazing neighborhoods across the city. Therefore, it was only necessary that we provided some popular neighborhoods that offer different lifestyles, from family-friendly communities to vibrant districts perfect for city living, and even rural areas just outside of Lisbon that offer a slower paced coastal living.

When you are living in Lisbon, you need to learn how to get around by using different modes of transport. Chapter 6 was dedicated to the different ways you can travel around the city as well as outside of the city, following some popular and scenic routes. When you are a tourist, it is vital that you learn how to use the different public transport systems as well as how to determine which mode of transport will be best for you and your itinerary. Lisbon has many options when it comes to public transport, and in this chapter we discussed the best options for you, but at the end of the day, we all learn that your own two feet will be the most reliable and useful way to move around the hilly city of Lisbon.

Transport is also important when planning your daily trips within the city as well as outside of the city. In Chapter 7, we explored the many destinations you can travel to when you are yearning for an outdoor adventure. The region outside of Lisbon offers some great hiking trails, surfing spots, as well as historical towns to explore. We provided a list of popular and unique day trip destinations that you can only experience once you take a scenic drive outside of Lisbon towards the coast or the mountainous villages for the perfect escape into nature.

While traveling around a charming and energetic city in Europe is a dream, we need to be practical about our health and safety, and never forget to be realistic when it comes to the current Covid-19 pandemic. In Chapter 8, we covered the basics of traveling during Covid-19 as well as the current Portuguese protocols and policies that need to be implemented within mainland Portugal. It is important to be observant and keep checking local news updates or official government websites about the present travel situation. Portugal has had many of its restrictions lifted, so many places are open to tourism, but remaining vigilant and remembering basic hygiene and public protocols will only make your trip around Lisbon easier and safer in the long run.

Lastly, Chapter 9 was dedicated to discussing the local lifestyle, culture, and customs of Lisbon. Here, we provided some tips on how to integrate into Lisbon society by connecting with the people of the city and learning more about the places you spend your time in. Being observant and adaptable are important when traveling around a foreign country or when you are planning to settle down in a new city. This is why we also broke down the unwritten social norms, dos and don'ts, as well as the local customs that you will need to become familiar with when living in Lisbon. There will be times when you will feel lost, overwhelmed, or out of place, but Lisbon and its people are friendly and will always welcome you to enjoy the magic and charm of this special city. It is up to you to get planning and get excited, and leave for Lisbon!

References

6 Things to do in lisbon in summer. (2022). Hotels. https://za.hotels.com/go/portugal/summer-things-to-do-lisbon

12 Months of festivals and events in lisbon. (2021, October 5). Lisbon Guru. https://www.lisbonguru.com/festivals-events-all-year-round/

Accommodations in lisbon. (2022). Booking.com. https://www.booking.com/accommodation/city/pt/lisbon.en-gb.html

Anna. (2019a, February 7). *Things to do during spring in lisbon*. Discover Walks Blog. https://www.discoverwalks.com/blog/things-to-do-during-spring-in-lisbon/

Anna. (2019b, December 12). *Top 9 streets to see in lisbon*. Discover Walks Blog. https://www.discoverwalks.com/blog/top-5-streets-see-lisbon/

Arrábida snorkeling adventure with transfer from lisbon. (2022). Tripadvisor. https://www.tripadvisor.com/AttractionProductReview-g189158-d13399433-Arrabida_Snorkeling_Adventure_with_Transfer_from_Lisbon-Lisbon_Lisbon_District_Cen.html

Ashley, E. (2020, January 8). *Lisbon on a budget: 25 travel tips for first-timers*. Mint Notion. https://www.mintnotion.com/travel/lisbon-travel-guide-on-a-budget/

Autumn in lisbon: activities to enjoy the city. (2020, September 24). Collegiate - PT. https://www.collegiate-ac.pt/en/student-news/autumn-lisbon/

Best neighbourhoods in lisbon for investors. (2019, April 20). Get Golden Visa. https://getgoldenvisa.com/best-neighbourhoods-in-lisbon-investors

Bloomidea. (2022). *The most iconic streets of lisbon*. Lisboa Cool. https://lisboacool.com/en/blog/the-most-iconic-streets-of-lisbon

Bon, R. (2018, March 28). *Lisbon travel guide: lovely things to do in spring*. Roselinde. https://www.roselinde.me/lisbon-travel-guide-things-to-do-spring/

Catarina. (2017, March 6). *6 Things to do in lisbon in the spring*. A Portuguese Affair. https://www.aportugueseaffair.com/lisbon-spring/

Christina. (2018, June 13). *Visit lisbon like a smartie: 9 silly mistakes you must avoid*. Happy to Wander. https://happytowander.com/visit-lisbon-mistakes/

Craig, S. (2021, September 19). *13 essential tips for traveling to lisbon on a budget*. History Fangirl. https://historyfangirl.com/travel-lisbon-on-a-budget-portugal/

Culture and social etiquette in portugal. (2021, March 21). Expat Guide to Portugal | Expatica. https://www.expatica.com/pt/living/integration/etiquette-in-portugal-106561/

Dube, R. (2022, March 7). *I traveled to lisbon and here are 20 tips I recommend for those who are interested in visiting this gorgeous city*. BuzzFeed. https://www.buzzfeed.com/racheldube/i-traveled-to-lisbon-and-here-are-20-tips-i-recommend-for

Edun, L. (2021, April 18). *Lisbon expat guide, Pt. 2: The best neighbourhoods for families*. Dispatcheseurope. https://dispatcheseurope.com/lisbon-expat-guide-pt-2-the-best-neighbourhoods-for-families/

Events. (2022). Visitlisboa. https://www.visitlisboa.com/en/events

Facebook, Instagram, LinkedIn, Twitter, & Instagram. (2020, October 29). *Getting around lisbon: guide to public transportation*. TripSavvy. https://www.tripsavvy.com/lisbon-public-transportation-guide-1642554

Food experiences in lisbon. (2022). Eatwith. https://www.eatwith.com/search?q=Lisbon%2C+Portugal

Giddings, P. (2022a). *Lisbon beaches; beach guide and best beach in 2022.* LisbonLisboaPortugal. https://lisbonlisboaportugal.com/lisbon-beaches.html

Giddings, P. (2022b). *Lisbon driving; the best driving routes, day trips with a car and car rental car guide.*

LisbonLisboaPortugal. https://lisbonlisboaportugal.com/lisbon-transport/Driving-in-Lisbon.html

Horanin, J. (2019, January 30). *Your practical guide to transportation in lisbon*. The Blond Travels. https://www.theblondtravels.com/transportation-lisbon/

Information, M. K. (2020, October 31). *How to make a travel itinerary*. Thebarefootnomad. https://www.thebarefootnomad.com/info/how-to-make-a-travel-itinerary/

Kristiansen, K. P. (2020, April 12). *Best neighbourhoods in lisbon for families*. Triple Passport. https://www.triplepassport.com/best-neighbourhoods-in-lisbon-for-families/

Lisbon hotels and places to stay. (2022). Tripadvisor. https://www.tripadvisor.co.za/Hotels-g189158-Lisbon_Lisbon_District_Central_Portugal-Hotels.html

Lisbon, portugal; a tourism guide for 2022. (2022). Lisbonlisboaportugal. https://lisbonlisboaportugal.com/index.html

Lisbon scenic drives. (2022). Enjoytravel. https://www.enjoytravel.com/en/travel-news/epic-road-trips/best-scenic-drives-near-lisbon

Lisbon to lagos by bus and train. (2022). Www.lagosportugalguide.com. https://www.lagosportugalguide.com/lagos-algarve/Lisbon-to-Lagos-bus.html

Lisbon Travel Guide. (2022). Nomadic Matt's Travel Site. https://www.nomadicmatt.com/travel-guides/portugal/lisbon/

Livingston, L. (2021, May 22). *Decoding lisbon: tips for visiting and avoiding tourist traps*. The Geographical Cure. https://www.thegeographicalcure.com/post/what-to-skip-in-lisbon

Lonely Planet. (2022). *Lisbon travel*. Lonely Planet. https://www.lonelyplanet.com/portugal/lisbon

Méndez, L. (2021, August 9). *8 Useful international travel tips for first-time travelers*. Gooverseas. https://www.gooverseas.com/blog/best-international-travel-tips-for-first-time-travelers

Pauline. (2022, February 23). *15 Lisbon travel tips to help you plan your trip to lisbon*. BeeLoved City. https://www.beelovedcity.com/lisbon-travel-tips

Pepper, L. (2022). *Cultural etiquette guide to lisbon*. Bbcgoodfood. https://www.bbcgoodfood.com/howto/guide/cultural-etiquette-guide-lisbon

Pettit, S. (2021, December 9). *The best neighborhoods to live in lisbon*. Expat Guide to Portugal | Expatica. https://www.expatica.com/pt/moving/location/best-neighborhoods-in-lisbon-1113902/

Portuguese Culture - Do's and Don'ts. (2022). Cultural Atlas. https://culturalatlas.sbs.com.au/portuguese-culture/portuguese-culture-do-s-and-don-ts

Restaurants in Lisbon. (2022). Tripadvisor. https://www.tripadvisor.co.za/Restaurants-g189158-Lisbon_Lisbon_District_Central_Portugal.html

Roobens. (2021, September 22). *Things to do in lisbon in winter.* Been around the Globe. https://www.beenaroundtheglobe.com/lisbon-in-winter/

Sales, G. (2022). *6 Tips for first-time travelers abroad.* GoAbroad. https://www.goabroad.com/articles/tips-for-traveling-abroad-first-time

Sander. (2017, May 17). *How to create the perfect travel itinerary In 8 simple steps.* Ars Currendi. https://www.arscurrendi.com/travel-itinerary/

Santos, N. (2017, October 30). *11 things tourists should never do in portugal, ever.* Culture Trip. https://theculturetrip.com/europe/portugal/articles/11-things-tourists-should-never-do-in-portugal-ever/

Schist villages of lousã mountain. (2022). Viator. https://www.viator.com/tours/Coimbra/Half-Day-Tour-from-Coimbra-to-Schist-Villages-of-Lousa-Mountain/d23421-88472P3

ShinyShiny, L. N. F. D. for E. -. (2019, June 4). *The 7 best beaches in lisbon to suit every taste.* Oliver's Travels. https://www.oliverstravels.com/blog/best-beaches-lisbon/

Silva, L. (2021a, November 25). *Lisbon.* Portugal. https://www.portugal.com/city/lisbon/

Silva, L. (2021b, November 25). *Lisbon*. Portugal. https://www.portugal.com/city/lisbon/

Stingy Nomads. (2019, May 22). *The portuguese camino de santiago- our detailed guide & itinerary*. Stingy Nomads. https://stingynomads.com/camino-portugues-stages/

Sylvia, A. (2020, March 30). *Lisbon travel tips: what you should know before visiting*. Wapiti Travel. https://www.wapititravel.com/blog/en/lisbon-travel-tips/

The 5 most beautiful streets in lisbon. (2020, November 19). Collegiate - PT. https://www.collegiate-ac.pt/en/student-news/beautiful-streets-lisbon/

The fátima walking route. (2022). Infatima. https://www.infatima.pt/en/plan-the-trip/pilgrimage/ways/the-fatima-walking-route#page-top

Time Out Lisbon. (2021, September 17). *Travel tips every lisbon visitor should know about*. Time out Lisbon. https://www.timeout.com/lisbon/things-to-do/tourist-survival-guide

Titova, J. (2017, June 28). *Adopt, adapt – cultural faux pas in portugal through the eyes of an expat*. Travel Tips and Concierge Service Blog. https://meetngreetme.com/blog/dos-donts-culture-in-portugal-expat-shares-advice/

Top 10 lisbon beaches. (2022). Lisbonbeachesguide. https://www.lisbonbeachesguide.com/top-10-lisbon-beaches.html

Top 11 annual events in lisbon. (n.d.). Inyourpocket. Retrieved May 18, 2022, from https://www.inyourpocket.com/lisbon/top-11-annual-events-in-lisbon_76640f

Top lisbon dining experiences. (2022). Viator. https://www.viator.com/Lisbon-tours/Dining-Experiences/d538-g6-c20

Visiting portugal? here are the best things to do in lisbon. (2022). Things to Do in Lisbon - Context Travel - Context Travel. https://www.contexttravel.com/blog/articles/things-to-do-in-lisbon

Image References

Evangelista, P. (2021). In *Unsplash.* https://unsplash.com/photos/Ss3FBqiWwP4

García, D. (2018). Walking around in lisbon. In *Unsplash.* https://unsplash.com/photos/CVZ0y7APRtU

Marcu, D. (2016). In *Unsplash.* https://unsplash.com/photos/Brj1YY8FoD4

Paganelli, A. (2019). The tower. In *Unsplash.* https://unsplash.com/photos/rYVmXecm64Q

Stan, C. (2020). Cascais waterfront and beach near lisbon, portugal. In *Unsplash.* https://unsplash.com/photos/1V-hH2oF3Is

www.ingramcontent.com/pod-product-compliance
Lightning Source LLC
Chambersburg PA
CBHW062116220526
45471CB00010B/3751